Dedicated to these who have targets

Ioannis Balis is from Hellas.
He originates from beautiful cities of Edessa and Tripolis,
his parents are George and Foteini Balis.
He lives in Koukaki of Athens.
He has studied computing science
he paints, writes poems and songs as well.
One of his favorite phrase that has as motivation in life is that man has to be like the road,
goes everywhere and when the road doesn' t leads nowhere then make your own road.

Why You Don't Laugh

Ioannis Balis

authorHOUSE®

AuthorHouse™ UK Ltd.
500 Avebury Boulevard
Central Milton Keynes, MK9 2BE
www.authorhouse.co.uk
Phone: 08001974150

First published by AuthorHouse 2/21/2011

ISBN: 978-1-4567-7302-1 (sc)

Any people depicted in stock imagery provided by Thinkstock are models, and such images are being used for illustrative purposes only. Certain stock imagery © Thinkstock.

This book is printed on acid-free paper.

Come on little Matt junior to tell you a story.

Says the woman in charge in the orphanage.

This story is about an old wealthy man and his family.

Especially family members that are tested by the old man.

Also this story involves and other men that are chosen by the wealthy man in order to do something for him.

He blackmails them.

Even the members of his family.

He is so wealthy that he doesn't care about spending money for persons that love.

He is working he is rich because of his work.

One day get rid of all.

He goes abroad and starts a new life.

But first of all, he directs his death and his funeral.

All are persuaded for his death.

Relatives and friends.

Also enemies.

When he left he also left unpaid bills, checks without money in bank accounts.

The name of this man is Robert.

He is tall with white hair.

Robert has a company that deals with inventions.

He has many threats and enemies. Ann is a jealous woman, she never likes what Roberts does and she never tells him a good word.

She is jealous of him because she never done anything by her own.

The couple has three children, Alan, Liza and Kevin.

Alan is working in his job company, Liza and Kevin too.

None of them want to do something like a business.

They used to make fun of the workers of the company they used to go late job, or not going at all.

One day Liza made sex with a worker and the other day said to all that this man raped her.

Robert fired this man from the job.

She said to her brothers that she would do it again.

She had take drugs that day of the fact and made sex with Alec the worker.

She used to take drugs, she is crazy, she spends money, she goes to parties every day and one day they found her in coma and transfer her to

Hospital in high she stayed for a few days and she was teasing the doctor Mark.

A young guy, tall with black hair.

Liza is in the telephone department.

She takes notes for her dad, or orders, from clients.

She does all the paper work.

Photocopies and all that stuff.

Kevin is in the testing department.

Alan is in the advertising department.

He always says that he wants to get in the testing department and that he is better than his brother.

He is not happy with his life he always wants something else and especially something that his brother has.

He is addicted to drugs like her sister.

He often takes the yacht of his father.

He goes trips without saying anything in nobody.

He almost kills himself ones, when he got drunk with a whore and passed with the boat very close to a rock.

He is blond.

Kevin is black hair and angry looking.

Ann is soft, so soft that somebody can say that she is silly.

Her relatives accuse Robert of not giving her chances to prove that she worth something.

Robert is not well enough lately.

Doctors suggested him not to get tired and not get anxiety.

Every day he has the same program.

He steps in the same spots, in pavement and road, and his yard, he never changes route to anywhere.

He goes everywhere through a specific route.

As if as he has a path.

He eats specific food, in specific places.

Ann, doesn't cook, she orders every day from a specific place.

Robert ate food from a woman's hand three days before his mother died.

From his mother.

His mother got poisoned.

25 years ago.

This family is strange.

The only thing that is not missing is the laugh.

Not they are clever People with clever humor but because each of them has made his own world and he laughs with things that thinks that are funny.

Many dramatic facts take place and many funny facts too.

But there are many confusions about which is funny and which is dramatic.

Alan has bad thoughts of people and always thinks what to do to have fun.

He always fined good things as he says in order to get high.

But after that he gets bored again.

The every day timetable involves plays with Alan Liza and Kevin .

Jokes and fights.

Threats from Robert that he wont' give them nothing from the money when he is dead and cries from Ann.

This scary comedy is a habit and for the neighbors

Robert lately is making an invention that looks like a game of mind.

His family asks him what is this but he never gives a straight answer.

Ann gets bored of him and says to children, get rid of this crazy.

Live your life.

In fact he didn't make it by his own.

A friend of him made that invention and sent it to him as a toy.

Robert made the order so now he tries to find the solution, not to create or finish the invention.

This invention consists of some doors.

The doors are small and closed to each other.

The person that plays with this invention and game of mind has to open all doors and none of the others is clocked.

The fact is that when you unlock another door is locked.

Someone has to try hard to open all doors without having locking another.

Robert is not as useful as in the past.

He doesn't want to admit that.

He gives his name in the inventions that the department makes.

The inventions aren't made of him.

Some ideas only.

He has put the invention in the living room.

Alan one day says it but he didn't pay any attention to that.

He looked at it and left.

Kevin looked at the invention and knock it down while he was going out drunk as he was.

The only truth that this family knows is that there is no respect between its members.

The image that is the only that is left from this family, Robert tries to keep it in the years that come.

It is difficult.

Each member live for him self.

Robert is in very difficult place.

He is tired of this life.

Especially of this family.

In his job he spend most of his time because he has motivation and some colleagues and superiors that like him.

They always tease him because his wife is very younger than him.

Some of them laugh at him behind him.

Only one girl likes him more than the others without wanting to make her job only or to take advantage of his sympathy to her.

Jenna.

A young blond well looking girl that is one of his secretaries.

Jenna works for him the last 5 years.

He is satisfied from her and also her.

Jenna is 25 years old.

She is well educated.

Liza is jealous of her.

She often makes jokes to her.

She insists of going out together.

Once she has threatened her that if they wouldn't go out together she would say that she is a lesbian.

This is the only truth that Jenna wants to hide from Robert.

Jenna is from a very serious family.

Her father is colonel and her mother a teacher in blind kids.

George and Karol.

Half Irish and half American.

Her brother is guard.

He always works at nights.

He has problem with going to toilet.

He can only go at nights.

But when his colleges shift done he is alone and he always want to go for crap when he is alone.

He has to drink coffee in order to keep him awake and the coffee causes him worse toilet problems.

His name is Tom.

But his colleagues call him crappie.

These two families have something common   .

The yards that are between their homes.

Robert and George have specific ways and manners.

They often do things to surprise one each other.

George says crazy Robert.

He often take electricity from Roberts home bills of Roberts family are very high.

Liza splits her gums in the way that her father passes and accuses Jenna for that.

Roberts shoes have gums above them.

Because they all teasing him he decide to make some fun of them.

He called his lawyer and his personal doctor.

Robbie and Mark.

He explains that he intends to disappear for a while.

He says that the is willing to be dead for his family and for all.

They advise him not to do it.

Both Robbie and Mark thinks of the company and the people that want to destroy it.

Meanwhile, Liza wants to work as a photographer, model, singer, create her own clothes and all things that she can't do.

First scene.

First day

First dialogue

First scenery

Robert with his car sawn leaving his home.

Camera saws him in the face and afterwards in his eyes.

He is anxious.

He goes to the company.

He gets in the parking.

He leaves the car to the guard to park it to the parking.

He gets of his car.

Second scene

The old man (black or white person with beard and not very well looking and dressed) sees him.

- Hello.

He says to him.

- Hello, how are you Jack what's up?

Robert tells him.

- Good

Jack replies.

- You always stink worse.

Robert is telling while he enters the building of his company.

R M company from his initials.

Third scene

Jim Cartal a man without self respect and confidence approach him.

- Eh hello Rob.

He is telling him Rob, because he believes that Roberts is a robber and steals the clients with the gadgets and invention that he sales.

- What do you want?

Robert reply's.

The two men speaking as the walk to the elevator.

Jim starts talking to Robert while he is standing on his shoulder.

Man I found a chick, a very good one yesterday.

It's your chance to suck something that worth Jim.

Not only me.

But a woman's body.

Robert tells him.

Man why are you so aggressive.

I don't like men who are aggressive.

Only women.

Jim tells him.

Jim is a man a little bulb underwear's glasses.

Ask them if they like you.

Robert tells him.

Fourth scene

The get in the elevator.

Liza gets out of it.

She is smiley.

Hello.

She says to both men as she almost fall down because she slept very late the night before.

Where are you going?

Robert asks her while Jim stays steel looking at her.

We live in silicone society my friend.

Says Jim.

Outside, can't live with all these poor guys up there.

Liza says and gone.

You eat because of them you silly girl.

Robert said to her.

A no, use of my terrific body.

She responses.

Hitting with her hand her ass.

Fifth scene

Nice chiks.

Jim says.

Sixth scene

Liza is going out.

Kevin arrives at job.

Is 10q00 o' clock.

Hey , are you going?

He tells her.

Far away.

She replies

And you bitch?

She tells him

To work.

He says laughing.

The truth is that I am going to hug your girlfriend.

She tells him.

You couldn't to get it up yesterday.

She has used to it yet.

As she told me.

She tells him.

What? what are you talking about bitch.

Come back here.

He shouts at her while she is living.

Seventh scene

Kevin is entering the building.

Camera shows his back and in the same time show Liza.

Liza is going to find Matt.

A junky.

She is out of drugs.

She takes the car (Luxury car)

And spinning the tires she goes.

Jack sees these two children.

Sort girl...

He wispers.

Sort girls have tall quality in bed my friend.

Sean says to him.

Sean is a cleaner.

He says lies and stories that invents.

He lives alone in a terraced house a poor district.

He is a little smart and have company with Jack several times.

He is a man that likes to steal ideas from others and thoughts.

Eight scene.

Liza finds Matt in a dark alley at his home.

Hello.

He tells him.

Come in.

He tells her.

I don't care if someone saw you we are not in a movie.

If something goes wrong, your dad has money.

Ha ha.

Liza smiles.

Liza seats in the sofa.

She crosses her legs.

Her skirt is going up.

She shows almost all her leg.

Matt.

Makes coffee.

He is handsome.

His hair is pony tail.

He wears jean and a t shirt without sleeves.

He can't look at her.

While he does it he turns from the other so to avoid looking at her.

He likes her.

But she is afraid of her too.

Don't be shy. Come seat next to me.

She tells him.

He goes to her ungry.

He grapes her from The neck.

You listen bitch, you know that i like you and you take advantage of that.

You come here whenever you want.

But I will put an end to that.

Liza sees her with joy and power as if she tells him that you are a week little man harmless and you can't do anything to me.

She looks him in the eyes.

She starts getting her skirts up.

I will let you have me.

They start kissing.

They lay in the sofa.

Matt starts undressing Liza.

The poorness will fuck the capitalism.

He says.

If you thinking like that i am going to live.

She replies.

Oh no my dear stay.

He says.

They start making sex.

Without condom.

Nineteen scene

Robert calls Max at his office.

Max comes.

Max gets into office.

Let have it.

Robert tells him.

How things go?

He asks him.

E…

Max hesitates.

(Max is the consultant of Robert, especially in finance aspects.).

Worse.

He says.

What do you mean?

Robert asks him

The sales has decreases 15%, the sales is decrease since last year 22% and since the last month 5%.

The suppliers are unpaid a few weeks now and the clients…

He stops.

Tell me.

Are held in phone for several minutes.

We have to pay salaries for 100 employers, 50 suppliers, 5 drivers, four secretaries and the bills.

We almost have enough money for the employers.

The employers in the creation department.

I mean.

Well what do you suggest?

Robert asks him.

Well i am afraid to make a suggestion any more.

Last year i have made one but you didn't listen to me.

I suggested not to hire 20 employers that liza wanted but...

He says.

Half of them were junkies and you know that Robert.

Half of them weren't coming at job and get paid without reason.

You are in big trouble.

You are right, I didn't hear you.

But now what can we do.

It was the thanks day then that's why I heard her.

Says Robert.

I' ill tell you.

The twenty employers that you hired haven't close year.

They can not demand for salary if you fire them.

I see

Well I will notify you.

Robert tells.

You do not have enough time.

As the days pas they will have rights.

You have to move fast, else they will laugh at you.

Max says.

Ok thank you.

Robert tell him.

Call my daughter.

He continues.

Somehow a letter is on Roberts desk when Max gone.

A yellow envelope.

Is on the office.

Tenth scene.

Robert take the envelope.

He invents to open that.

Robert has a problem.

He sweats easily.

In the same time Max call him.

Liza is not in the building.

He tells him.

Ok Max, thank you.

Meanwhile Liza and Matt have finished.

Eleventh scene

Oahu, this is the first time I slept with rich girl.

Matt says.

How was it?

Liza asks him.

Rich sex.

He says

And both of them laugh.

Well, give me the peels now, you know I run out of them.

Liza tells him.

They cost, you know.

He tells her.

I have money.

She says to him.

And I because of you doll.

He replies.

He give her a bag.

You have to do me a better price.

You had sex with me.

She says to her.

Ha ha.

That' s why god made man and woman, to have joy with each other, dol.

You will pay every pen of that I want.

He says.

Now that you fucked me you don't care e?

Ok.

How much do you want asshole?

I have money.

She says to him.

You may have, but rich human depend on guys like us to do their business, if I don't give you drugs where else can you find.

Nowhere, you afraid of the places with the drugs, you only can come to me.

If I don't give you, you will die.

Well is 100 green.

Liza through him the money that have not in appropriate place in her bag around her things and leaves fast pulling her dress in anger. Matt left home laughing.

Mean while

Twelve scene

Ann is at home.

She cleans the house.

She bends over Alan's bed which is in the same room as his brother and sister and she sees something.

While she is mopping under the bed she found something that looks like a crypt.

Under the children room is the living room.

But Ann doesn't pay attention and she continues mopping.

She thinks that the floor is damaged there.

It's 17:00 o' clock.

The two children arrive home.

Liza is still outside.

Robert also.

Ann hears noises at the ground floor and going downstairs.

-    Hello my boys. How was your day?

Ann says.

-    Boring.

Says Alan.

-    Exhausting.

Says Kevin without believing that.

What do you prepared to eat?

Alan asks Ann.

I was waiting you. I was about to cook today.

She replies.

Yes but now is late.

You should have prepared something.

Alan tells Ann.

It is never late for an egg you idiot.

Kevin tells him and laugh making joke at her mother.

Thirteen scene

Ann goes to the kitchen.

Wash your hands and seat to the table.

We will eat.

But where is Liza?

Who cares?

Kevin says.

With someone. or somebody.

Alan says laughing at her sister.

I mean that her taste to men is not good.

He continues.

After a few minutes Liza comes.

Fourteen scene.

She run toward her room.

She gets worse.

Kevin says.

Alan and Kevin laugh.

She has money, what else she wants.

Alan says.

When you are rich and especially rich bitch you can buy everything but not a human

Kevin tells him.

No my friend, that's why there are whores.

They are human beings belongings to someone.

Ann node like she aggress with Alan.

Life confuses you all the time.

To do this or that, or the other one.

All the time you have dilemmas and wondering what is right or wrong.

I am bored of this life.

Alan says.

The two children looking each other.

Means while.

In the RM company. (Robert Morison).

Fifteen scene

Robert orders for a coffee because he avoids drinking coffee at mornings.

Jinna a secretary fetches him the coffee.

Bob a clever employer that works in creation department near Robert's office make complaints to Jinna.

I am here 5 years, and he has never asked for my opinion, looks like I am not working here.

All ideas of him are worthless and not good tested in order to be in the trade.

But don't understand that.

Why does he have this policy?

He tells her.

He is odd you know that, nowadays he has financial problems as far as I understood
She tells him

Meanwhile.

Robert at his office calls Jim.

Sixteen scene.

Bring me the statistics and the accounts.

He tells him.

Robert puts the yellow envelope in his cupboard.

He drinks a little from his coffee.

French coffee, in my company.

He whispers.

He prefers the American products .

Jim is knocking Robert's door.

Robert makes Jim waits.

After a few seconds.

He says.

Come in.

I brought the papers that you asked for.

And the checks that we have given to suppliers and employers.

Robert at the same time have a an external call.

-Who is it?

He says

Is mister Lukas the minister.

Jinna says.

O what again.

He had helped me once and he probably wants a favor.

Give me him. Hello, George, how are you?

What can I do for you?

Well you I can, we live in country of hire and paying for all.

Ok thank you.

Bye.

Robert closes the phone

Well Jim, the things are not so good.

I think of disappearing for a while.

Robert says.

Another call is for Robert.

His phone is ringing.

Jina wants to transfer him a phone call.

- I told you not to be bothered.

He tells her with angry way and closes the phone.

Seventeenth scene

- But when did he said that?

She wonders.

Ann he can't talk at the moment.

I will tell him to call you when he is not busy.

Thank you.

- What a family.

She says after closing the phone.

Eighteenth scene

As I can se there is a mistake there.

When we bought iron we pay 10% more expensive than a month ago.

This is very odd if we see the last agreement and the contract with the G note company of Sam Goldrow.

The amount that we have ordered is biger than the first order and in the last two months we had an incensement as you have told me.

Robert says.

No, but how can you say that.

The papers are speaking by themselves.

I didn't anything for incensement.

There was a lack in the conversation.

Jim says.

What lack I am not fool.

I know that nobody here likes me.

But I will an end to that.

Robert says.

He gets up.

He starts sweats

This is something wrong with the gross.

Jim says.

We live in planet of sales and I don't have salesmen.

Robert says.

The problem is not the sales.

Is that there is a lack of ideas.

Jim says.

Nineteenth scene

Robert looking from the window.

What do you mean ?

I don't have ideas?

Robert says.

Jim is laughing

Come on now Robert, you know that your ideas don't feat anymore.

Jim says.

What about that bookshop in Maryland.

You made a machine that can shows to you the most important things in each page.

You have sale 1000 of that thing, but afterwards somebody I don't know how make the same too.

He sold that cheaper and trough you out of market.

Your problem is that you don't hat you don't have reliable colleges.

Something that you let to be done.

Jim says.

Let me see the income and the expenses.

Robert says.

According to this chart gadgets should advertise more.

In these 5 states you earned more than the other 10, because of good promoting.

These gadgets you have sold there were almost useless than you promises, but people bought them.

Jim says.

I asked you to tell me the income.

Robert says.

Ok ok. You earned 50.000 dollars.

Jim says.

What?

What are you talking about?

50.000

I won't have money to pay the employers.

Robert says.

E, e you give the less money from all the competitors of you.

Ha ha.

Jim says.

You have to know that your wife and daughter have passes the twelve in Caribbean in the company expenses.

Jim continues.

O shit.

But she that I can not do that in this specific company.

I can not put as expensive the personal expenses of my family or me myself.

Jim is laughing.

Women.

Women.

He says.

I want you to know that you want 20.000 more in order to pay all your staff.

Ok. Thank you, Jim, let me think what I will do.

Robert says to Jim and Jim .

Robert seats in his seat.

If I have face lifting.

If I disappear, my family doesn't support me.

My colleges are not with me in difficult days and someone makes bad in my company.

If I leave they may understand how important I am.

He opens his cupboard.

He reads the letter.

The letter is from an unknown person to him.

From Michael Newman.

An English doctor.

I want to buy your home in , but I want some time to think of your offer.

I don't have all the money now, but I can give you the first dose of 20.000.

We have to sign the contracts if you want to procceed.

Robert calls him at once.

Mr Newman please.

He says.

Yes it's me.

Are you Mr Morison

Newman says.

Yes it's me.

I call ed you in order to meet each other, to discuss about the home.

Robert Morison has a home in Manhattan that none of his relatives know that exists.

He intents to sale it so to get some money.

Ok, when can you?

Newman asks Roberts when he can.

Let's say about tomorrow in the Lalo cage?

Robert says.

That's Ok.

At what time?

Newman says.

Is it good for you at 1000?

Robert asks.

Yes that's fine.

Newman says.

Newman is a fat and tall guy with moustache and black hair

He took pension .

He was working as worker in mine.

Meanwhile.

Twentieth scene.

Tom is leaving from his home.

He sees Liza crying at her bedroom that is in the second floor of Morison home.

He tries to say hello to her.

He falls onto a trash can.

He makes noise.

Liza starts laughing.

Hello.

Tom is telling to her.

Liza nodes her hand as if she says hello and get in her again.

I like her, but it' difficult to have her.

Tom whispers as he goes to work.

Twenty first scene

Liza make a call to an agent that she found in internet.

This agent has in his site the title use, we product actors and shows.

Hello, are you Vick?

Liza says

Every inch of me and I have a lot of inches.

He replies.

Well I called you because I want you to see me...

Vick is agent especially for young foolish girls ambitious to do it all in order to be famous and earn money and everything else.

He is young, he has crazy attitude and style, and color of hair.

She tells him.

And everything you want.

He replies.

Well ha ha.

When and how can I see you?

She asks her.

E just a moment to see my schedule doll.

He says.

Twenty third scene.

He look's at his empty calendar.

Well today I can't

Not tomorrow.

Well , I am busy all this week.

Let's for the next.

He tells her.

A, ok.

The sooner that you can, I believe I am talented.

She says to him.

I know you are.

He replies.

But how?

She ass smiling.

I can recognize that from the voice.

He says smiling.

You are funny guy.

She tells him.

Well, you will find out what else I am.

He tells her smiling.

Twenty forth scene.

Ann is kinking Lisa's door.

Liza.

She says.

Oh, my mother sweet voice.

Liza to Vick.

I have to close.

She continues.

Ok.

Vick says.

See you.

Liza says and close laughing and happy.

Twenty fifth scene.

Another one free chick.

Vick says and claps his hands.

Twenty sixth scene

What again?

Liza says.

You haven't eat.

Ann tells her.

I am not in the mood.

Liza replies.

Ann opens the whole door as she was looking inside while it was a little opened and gets into the room.

But why? What happened?

Ann asks Liza.

And seats in the bed near her daughter.

Well mum, I seek of that life.

I am seek of waiting money from dad.

I want my own.

Liza says.

But you have it all.

Ann tells her.

Yes but life is too easy for me.

I want to do things.

To know people.

To be a star.

I am rich, money is the bigger talent nowadays.

Wake up mum.

Liza says.

O come on, I will talk to him to give you more money.

Ann says.

Now come downstairs to eat something.

Ann tells her.

No I am ok, thanks, I love you mam.

Liza says.

Me too.

Ann says.

Liza intents to start diet in order to be nice in front of Vick.

Although she doesn't have problem with her body.

Twenty seventh scene

Meanwhile

Kevin is sleeping in the couch.

Ann puts caramels of lemon to his food instead of lemon because he run out of that.

Ann is looking at him.

What are you doing?

She says angry.

We are out of lemons you know.

And I want lemon for my food.

But these have sweet taste.

Ann tells him.

Let me have something in my life.

He tells her, he takes the plate with the food and goes to the room in which is Liza.

Meanwhile Robert is coming home.

Twenty eight scene

He meet by change Tom.

Eh Tom where, are you going?

Robert says to Tom.

Fine Mr. Morison, I am going to work.

He responds.

How is your father.

Robert says father instead of father in purpose.

He starts laughing but hide his smile.

Tom didn't understand the teasing of mister Robert.

E, e he is good you.

Robert is parking his parking.

Tom's father is seeing Robert from his window.

The night has fallen.

Every creature is going to sleep.

But Liza is laying in her bed with her eyes open.

She is waiting for something.

Alan is sleeping with his pie in his mouth.

Kevin hasn't change position and still sleeping in the couch.

Twenty ninth scene

The next morning Robert is going to Lalo's cafe.

There is a fat tall guy that seems to be Newman.

He approaches very carefully looking around him.

He doesn't trust anyone.

He is afraid that envy relatives could harm him.

Eh it's me Newman.

Come on my friend I don't byte .

Newman tells Robert.

Oh. are you Mr. Newman.

Robert asks.

The tow en make a handsake.

Afterwards be seated.

Well let's see which deal we can have.

Newman says.

I have decided to give you 30.000.

I am interested for this house.

I want to buy it.

Newman says.

Ok, but it's a little odd because you haven't seen it inside.

Robert says to him.

Well I imagine that the home is good enough, I know that a businessman had it before, I mean you, ha and also that it wound be clean and painted.

Newman says.

Are you sure that you don't want to see it?

Robert asks.

Is there a problem Mr. Morison?

Are you sure that you want to sell this home?

Newman responds.

Robert starts sweating.

No, No.

He says.

A, are you married?

Newman asks Robert.

A lot.

Robert replies.

Women, women.

If you see another's woman nice ass, they will tell you, a why you are looking at her, at this a that.

But they always look their asses in the mirror to see if they are nice looking to public.

They are crazy

Simple crazy..

Thirty scene

Meanwhile Tessa the waitress arrives.

Speak of the devil Mr. Morison.

Asses, Ha, the most dirty but the better thing in woman's body.

Do you agree?

Ha.

Newman says.

Well when I am dieing I prefer to be inside one of them.

Ha.

He continues.

Robert doesn't talk.

Bring us the usual that I take.

If you don't mine Mr. Newman.

These have good taste.

Twenty ninth scene.

(Meaning the coffees).

Mr. Newman nodes as it is ok with that.

You are very puritan Mr. Morison.

Do you miss the joy in your life?

Come with me one night and be sure that I will make you smile.

You know sometimes the simple smile is stronger than a laugh.

You can have more joy in a smile than a laughing.

Newman says.

I am tired, that's all.

Robert replies.

Which is your lucky number Mr. Morison?

Newman asks.

You better have asked me if I have luck.

Robert replies.

Mine is 16 and 9, but especially the double numbers and these that have curves.

That's why I want to give you 30.000.

I believe that it will bring me luck.

He says.

Well I don't believe so the numbers but only the numbers that are products of work.

If you get my point.

Robert replies.

Thirty first scene.

The waitress brings the coffees.

Robert drinks slowly.

You are not a man of danger, e Mr. Morison?

Newman says to Robert.

I'd prefer looking the contracts instead of discussing what am I or not.

Robert says.

Oh, the wolf is showing his teeth.

Ok.

Well, read that contract.

Sign it and I will sign it too.

Robert says to Newman.

Ok.

You know that after we sign we can not regret.

Newman says.

We can, but we have to give the double money back.

Robert says.

Newman doesn't read the contract properly.

Thirty second scene.

300.000 total.

Ok Mr. Morison.

It's a deal.

Newman says.

Newman sign the contract.

Afterwards he pull from his black leather bag the block with checks.

He writes the bank check and give it to Robert.

You can take the money today.

He tells Robert.

Thirty three scene.

Robert is taking the check.

He is looking at it through his glasses.

- You have to put a little adventure your life Mr. Morison.

Newman says to Robert as he speaks to him as Robert is his superior or a very younger close friend of him.

- You may have right, but I am not so young now to do it.

Robert reolys.

- When you put a plant in the top of the hill it's your problem to get it's fruits from there so to gain something.

Newman says to him.

- What do you mean?

Robert asks him

- I mean that you could make your life different.

Newman tells him.

- Life is like a boat sometimes, it you everywhere it wants.

Robert replies to him.

- I agree, but of the times you have the wheal.

Newman says to him.

Robert looks at his watch.

- Well I have to go.

Robert says.

- You barely drunk your coffee.

Newman tells him.

- I usually drink my coffee that way, quickly.

He replies to him.

- Quick coffee, quick life.

Newman replies.

Robert gets up.

- What are you gonna do now?

He tells newman.

- I am gonna sit here for a while.

I don't have anything else to do do.

Siting a little here afterwards somewhere else and it goes on.

He says to Robert.

- I am jelus of you.

Robert tells him.

Newman is still siting.

- You are jelus of me?

You have it all my friend.

Money, company, boat, a luxury car that brought you HERE (HE SHOWS HIM THE CAR)
and family.

Newman says to him.

- Family, e? Do I?

Robert replies.

He nodes his hand as he say goobye and leaves.

He doesn't car if newman told him goodbye he has started looking down in the pavement or elsewhere but not up, who cares, he doesn't even.

Therty forth scene.

Robert goes to his company.

He looks at the table of the building.

Rm gudgets & inventions.

He laughs.

Jack sees him, he is ill and he can not speak.

Jim sees Robert too.

- E come on man.

He tells him.

- Come to tell you about yesterday.

I met a girl...

And he is talking until they get into the lift.

Thirty fifth scene

Meanwhile Liza is testing her vocal skills.

- Aaaaaaaaaa oooooooooooooooo eeeeeeee eoe.

She says.

She is till at home.

Alan has his day off today.

Kevin is on his road to job.

Ann tries for the first time to cook.

She reads a book for cooking.

- Oooo, ypu silly bitch, you ' ll never be a singer, the only thing that you can see

is to be the bitch of matcho and drug guys.

Alan tells her.

- O yeah.

Well I will prove you the opposite.

- Oh shut up.

Alan says her.

- One day you have to search for my photograph because I would have been famous.

Liza tells him.

- Well it is not a difficult issue.

I could find your photos in for him magazine.

And I have already told you that a lot of times, don't let the window open the nigths.

Now is a bee in the room and I have to fall on my knees so to get it.

He tells her.

- Try that once you may like it.

She replies him.

Tthirty fifth scene

Meanwhile Robert watch the route of dust coming from the window.

- Oh I forgot the check..

He calls Jenna to his office.

She is knocking the door and comes in.

- Yes Mr. Morison.

Ii it something that I can do for us?

She tells him.

- That's why I' ve called you.

He replies her with unger.

- Give this check to Jim to deposit in my personal account.

Not in the company's account.

- Okey sir.

Jenna says and goes.

- Summers go like the birds so to know other warms places.

In this way friends gone too.

The difference between animals and people is that animals know their enemy, instead of people that they could make handshake withsome one although he may betray
them.

Robert says alone in his office.

Thirty sixth scene

George soeaks with newman.

- Well what about the home, did he take the money, have you made the contract?

George asks him.

- Yes everything uder the plan.

But what you could earn with this story.

You could ruined the carreer of someone... but.

Newman tells him.

- Let these shit away.

Despite that you 've been my co employer for a while in the army, we planed this

story to get some money.

For different reasons.

I want to ruine him so my brother get into this business without competion and

you, and you to give some money for the elections of loukas to be elected.

Karol overhear the conversation while Tom their son is about to wake up to drink his coffee.

The conversation between the two men is ended.

Thirty seventh scene

- With whom you was talking my dear.

Carol asks George.

- With a friend from homeland my bear... eh dear.

He laughs at her.

- A, with whom?

She asks him.

- With Austin.

He tells her.

- Austin, I thougth he was deaf.

Ha ha ha.

She says

Austin was a friend of the couple but he died three months ago.

George knows that.

Tom also.

Tom was in the funeral.

George told Tom not to go to the funeral because many of the relatives of Austin acused George that caused the death of Austin by send him at home a striper.

Austin had make sex with her while her wife was abroad to her parents.

This striper had AIDS AND because the society was very closed this fact was well known.

Carol doesn't know that.

Tom undrestood that his father wants to hide something.

HE DOESN' T BELIEVE THAT THERE IS ANOTHER WOMAN IN HIS FATHER' S LIFE BUT SOMETHING ELSE STRANGE.
- AND WHERe IS HE NOW?
TOM ASKS HIM.
George doesn' t answer.
- You can not charge for the bullshit.
Tom sais.
- e tom, don' t speak like that.
I am going to school now.
Buy.
Carol sais.

Thirty-eighth SCENE

Mean while Robert has called Robbie, mark and max.
- the biggest thing in business is to export.
If a company is worth and doesn't' t make exportation is nothing.
- why do you tell that.
Robbie asks.
- It is so sure like the letters in translated films that are white.
Robert sais.
- i call you for a specific reason.
I inted to leave for a while.
- i don' t know when excactly but i will notify you.
If you have anything to tell me i can hear you.
Robert sais.
Max doesn' t talk.
He is sitting as he is guilty of something.
- but who is going to be in charge for the supplies?
Max tells him.
- I will notify you about this max, don' t worry.
Robert replies.
- I would like to know that, to see if he will be trustful.
Max sais.
- well I believe that all in our company are trustfull max.
Robert sais to him.
- no no no, mister morison, every man that deals with money is a little corapted, be care-
ful.
Max replies.
- ok max I got your point.
Robert sais to him.
Meanwhile jenna calls Robert.
- mister morison excuse me.
She sais.
- don' t say excuse, you are doing your job.
Tell me.
He sais to her.
- mister viewing is necessary to go at his office, there is a line from the bank for him.
Jenna sais.
Jenna means max.
- ok.
Robert sais.
- max there is bank in the line for you.
It is better to go at your office.
They may need something.
- ok mister morison, I go thank you.

- i have something to tell you robert.
Mark sais.
- let me have it.
Robert replys.
- it have been a lot of time that you have examinations.
I believe that it is about to do.
Mark sais.
- i feel like...
Robert sais.
- like a bull?
Sais mark.
- no, like two bulls.
Robert sais.
- ok, as you want, i wish you be that for ever.
Mark sais to him.
- aaaa, not for ever, and how you will earn...
Robert tels him.
- ha ha.
Mark laughs.
- now i have to go i have operation.
Mark sais.
- remind me your cell phone, to call you whenever i have time for you to come, i have already time for you, but just in case.
I always forget it.
Mark sais.
- you always forget it because i don' t have one.
 i believe that because of tecnologhy we don' t talk to each other.
Since the cell phones are invented.
I will call you if i need you, buy.
- As another example i can tell you the automotic laders that man invented in order not to walk, but he many times preferes the steps intead.
Robert sais to robie that he is still in robert' s office.
- it is another one of your habbits.
Robbie tells him.
Thertynine scene.

Liza calls jenna in the internal phone.
Bob answer the phone because jenna isn' t there.
- hello.
Bob sais.
- why you answer the phone?
Liza sais ungry.
- Jenna isn' t here at the...
He was about to say moment.
Liza close the phone.

- bitch.
Bob sais.

Forty scene.
- bitch e?
Liza sais behind bob' s back.
Bob is surprised.
He turns.
- but...
He sais.
- well to forget that i heared there is one thing that you can do, i don' t believe that you can acoplish that, but i wait you downstairs in women toilets.
You know that if i say to my dad anything he will believe me, so it' s you decision, what you will do.
- you would be my next victim.
She whispers while she goes downstairs.
Liza is not good, she run out of drugs.

Fortyfirst scene.

She goes to women toilets but she make vomit.
She goes from the job after that.
Jack sees her and gets up.
After a fiew minutes bob goes to toilets and he doesn' t see her there.
- she regrets that, better for me, she must have sicknesses.
Bob sais.

Fortysecond scene.

- Things are not going well.
I will leave the leadership of the company to you.
Robert sais to robbie.
- when did you desided that?
Robert line is ringing.
- yes.
Robert sais.
- yes it is me, jack, i saw your daughter liza leaving fast the company.
I think she is not fine.
Jack sais.
- ok thank you jack.
Robert sais.
- robbie i have to leave.
I am leaving this green envelope here next to my newspaper, there are some statistics and papers of max that I collected, some day I will ask you to have this envelope for some reason.

Robert sais.
- ok there is no problem, is anything that i can do to help you?
Robbie sasi to him.
- i believe no, everything i do i fell alone.
Robert sais and goes.

Fortythird scene.

The same time he bump into jim.
- ey, man.
Jim sais.
As if he sais to robert to be careful.
- what about the check?
Robert asks him.
- o man i almost got killed.
Before i got to the bank a car almost hit me with its fender.
A fat man was in it, he may had followed me.
Jim sais.
- ok. I have to leave now.
Robert sais to him.
- he left without asking me if i am fine.
Jim tells without thinking anything else.
Because he is interested about his health.
Robert leaves because he is interested about his daughter life.
He goes and buys a cell phone and send his phone number to the company by fax.
Robert goes at his home.

Fortyfourth scene.

He walks in the same path as every day, he looks at the same places as always.
In the flower shop of his area, and at the kiosk.
He lights a candle in the church of his area as every day.
He got at his home he is walking at the path that is in the garden between the lights.
He sees liza that is parking her car fast and get off it.
She throws her gum of the window.
Robert approaches.
- oh shit.
He sais.
He is stepping on the gums.
 He gets into the home.
He sees her fallen down in coma.
Allan is not at home.
The yacht isn' t outside.
Every time that the yacht isn' t there Alan has taken that.

Meanwhile.
Forty fifth scene.

Alan makes a turn with the yacht and scratch it in a rock.
- oh shit, i almost crashed it.
He sais.
He calls his mother.
- ey mom.
I am with the yacht i found a beautiful place here in Miami, I intend to spend some days here.
He sais to her.
- and what about your father, he will be mad when he finds out that.
Ann sais.
- I don' t care I want to do my life as he did too.
Don' t forget that he inherit a big fortune from his father in spite of he is telling that he is self created.
I have to switched off now.
He tells him and close the phone.
Alan is going with the yacht toward the beach.
He sees Sue a young blond girl.
He doesn't' t pretend the rich man.
But even though she doesn't' t look at him at all.
After a while they are sawn to play rackets.
But in a few minutes later they have a argue.

Meanwhile.
Forty-sixth scene.

Ann and Robert bring Liza to hospital.
Robert talks with mark.
- The fact is that the man uses the mind him only 10%
But the best thing is that there are many people that they use their stupidity only as the others intelligence only 10%.
This is good for other's people life.
Robert sais to mark.
- o come on Robert don' t tell that for your daughter.
Mark sais to Robert.
- i don' t tell that for my daughter but for the medical science.
I am here so long and i don' t know what Liza has.
Robert sais.
- o come on Robert you are here only a quarter.
We have made the appropriate examinations and we were waiting for the results.
I will tell you all you need.
Your daughter wasn' t eat enough.
Mark sais.

- that' s why she felt in coma?
Robert sais.
- no Robert, no, i wish that would be the cause.
Your daughter uses peals.
Mark sais.
- what?
Robert sais.
- she uses drugs Robert.
In fact she is addicted to them.
Mark sais to Robert.
- he has to be here fro a few days.
Mark sais.
- can i see her.
Robert tells him.
- no, she is been tested by my team now.
I will notify you.
- ok thank you for all.
Ann sees mark in the eyes.
Robert tells him and goes with ann.
He walks alone forward and Ann follows him.

Forty-seventh scene.

The next morning Liza is better, mark is in her room.
- Mister doctor.
She says in sexual way.
- come closer.
She says.
- how are you today?
Mark asks her.
- ready for all.
She replies.
There are six days before the meeting with Vick the agent.
- I will come back to you in a few minutes.
Mark tells her.
Liza turns on the TV.
She sees in news that a girl was found dead in Miami beach.
She was sawn lately with a young guy playing with rackets.
She calls her parents.
- E dad how are you?
She tells him.
- I try to put gums off my shoes.
He tells her.
- Dad Jenna did that.
Liza tells her.

- never mind, who cares for that now.
Are you better?
He tells her.
- Yes tomorrow I will be out.
She tells her.

Forty-eighth scene.

George is steeling electricity again.
Carol sees him.

FORTYNINTH scene

Liza wants to leave from the hospital.
6 days left before she will meet Vick.

Scene

Robert is at home for a while.
This is the first time that he sees his home and how it is.
A big cottage home with garden and parking.
George is bending to a tree
Kevin is seeing him.
-    E dad, what mister George is doing?

    Kevin asks his father.

-    A he is trying to steel some electricity.

    Robert replies.

-    And you tell that so easily, why don' t you do something.

    Kevin asks him.

-    Don' t be bothered with birdshit.

    Robert tells him.

-    Birdshit can ruin the color of a car dad.

    Kevin replies.

-    Ha ha, You may have right.

    Robert tells him.

    Robert has left a box downstairs next to the ladder.

- What is that in the ladder dad.

  Kevin asks.

- A something not important, a gadget.

  Robert sais.

- Ha ha. Okay.

  Kevin sais.

- But where is Alan and what about Liza is she okay?

  He asks.

- Liza is better than Alan.

  Robert replies and laughs.

- Liza will be out at six days.

  Robert says.

- I realy can' t find the reason why liza did it to her self.

  Robert says.

- Women dad, women.

  Kevin says.

- You know, I believe tha god made the misuraments and wieight and height just to bother the human beens.

  Kevin continues.

- I think you are right, in you age I was believing on that too..

  Robert says.

- Now?

  Kevin asks him.

- Now, I believe that the weight of your mom is the right mesurament, I haven' t seen another woman naked and so close to me since many years.

  Ha ha ha.

  Both of them laugh.

- Ok dad, I have to leave.

Bay bay.

Kevin says.

- Bay bay my son.

Be careful.

Robert replies.

Kevin is a little drunk but he hides it from his father, he pretends he is okay.

He goes downstairs and kick by mistake the box and he goes to job.

It falls down softly and as it is raped with paper it doesn't' t make noise.

Scene

Robert sees his watch.

He goes in every birthday of his employers.

Today bob has birthday.

He is been perpetrated while Ann is out for shopping.

She intend to cook for the first time, she seems that this time is determined to do it.

Robert is calling bob.

He always calls his employers by himself, he doesn't' t tell to others to call them for him despite some other businessmen.

scene

- Hello bob, happy birthday.

Robert sais.

- A, yes hello mister Morison, thank you very much.

Bob replies.

- Happy birthday.

  Robert says.

- I didn't have time today to see you that's why I called you.

  Robert says.

- O thank you very much mister morison.

  I am very glad that you called me.

  Bob says.

- We have to have a good releationship bob, we are human beings.

  Robert says.

- Yes I agree.

  Bob replies.

- Okay, see you at job.

  Robert says.

- Bay bay mister morison.

  Bob says.

- He always harry when he talks with me.

  Bob says.

  But why he doesn't like me?

  Bob says.

- Never mind.

  He says.

  Meanwhile.

  Robert gets out of his home to go to hospital.

  But his agenta falls down on the ground.

  Robert doesn't realize that and keep walking.

  He is going towards his car.

The agenta felt in front of geroege feets that was near.

He meets Tom close to his house.

Tom has rent two movies.

Robert sees the dvds.

Both tom and Robert likes movies.

-   Ey good morning tom.

    Robert sais.

-   Good morning mister Morison.

Tom and Robert are discussing.

-   If I were a move I would be a new and modern one.

    Tom says.

-   Yes but you know, a few people trust the new movies and less than the few will watch a new movie.

    Robert replies.

    He puts out of his pocket two little calendars.

-   Ey tell me when do you have birthday.

    Robert tells tom.

-   And why is that?

    Tom asks him.

-   Because I want to rent a movie for you, an old one, a classic, one that I prefer.

    If I were a movie, I would be an old and tested movie, trusted by most of the people.

    Robert says.

-   Bay bay for now I have to leave.

    Robert says and leaves while he lefts tom a little angry.

Meanwhile
George is calling Michael Newman.

- I passed close to that damn dog.

He sais.

Carol is near him.

- Did you kill it?

Newman asks him saying it referring to jim cartal.

- No. it was lucky.

George replies.

- Oh shit, we have problem now.

Newman replies.

- No, don' t worry.

George sais.

- I shoud have gone there to do this.

Newman sais.

- Ooo man.

We will start threatening him.

George says.

I will do it soon, I have to think what I shall say.

We will talk later.

George says.

Scene

Alan is talking with sue.

- How many personalities you have?

She asks him.

- One, the best.

He replies.

- Why are you telling me that, because I have tow cell phones?

  The one is for business and the other is my private one.

  He says.

- Well I have been told again these.

  She says.

  She is going faster than him, but he catches her.

- Why are you leaving?

  Come back to discuss it.

- No I am bored.

  She replies.

  This word makes alan realy angry.

  In a few minutes both of them can not been sawn by nobody.

Scene

After returning from hospital Robert goes to the company.

Robert goes at his office

He overhear Jenna speaking very sweet to someone on the phone.

She is speaking to her girlfriend.

When she sees Robert she is changes the sound of her voice.

He is fed up with everything, he is not man with anger and jelusy, he is calm but he wants to say that he feels, he is tired to keep his emotions.

In addition he has sense of humour too.

He approaches jenna.

- Jenna I know you, I know how to reialise if someone is straight or not, in all circumstances, so don' t pretend, I don' t have problem with your sexual affairs.

  He tells her.

She is standing with the telephone on her hand speechless.

Robert is getting in his office.

Jenna hungs up.

She goes fastt to robert' s office.

She knocks the door.

- Yes.

Robert says.

Jenna opens the door a little bit.

- Can i?

Jenna says.

- Yes it' s okay you can pass.

He replies.

- Mister Morison, how you know that?

Jenna says.

- What?

Robert relies.

- That, that I am a lesbian.

Jenna says.

- I know because you told me that Jenna.

She is speechless again.

She stays with her mouth open.

- Ha ha.

Robert laughs.

- And what about these that you told me outside?

Jenna tells him.

- Well Jenna I have decided to say that I feel.

Robert replies.

The same time Jim cartal knocks the door and opens it.

- O, excuse me, can I pass?

    He says.

- You have already done, it.

    Robert says.

- Wait me two minutes.

    Robert tells Jim.

- Ok thank you.

    Jim says and closes the door again.

- Well jenna you are a few years in the company, I don' t have problem with you.

    I intend to leave for a while.

    He tells her.

- I want you to watch everything.

    My daughter now is at hospital, alan will propably come at the end of the week and kevin is the next person after me in the leadership, the reason is because he is the most days at job.

    Robert has never made something like protocol for the next president in the company.

    There have to be elections for the replicate.

- Ha ha, it is a little odd because I told you my only secret.

    I told you that so easily as if you are a frined of mie.

    She says.

- That' s must be the relationship between an employer and an employee.

    Robert says.

    Robert is not testing how trustful is jenna and all the staff he know that in a company there are always talking and friendhips.

    He may has other reasons.

    Ann is calling him.

- Hello.

  He says.

- Hello.

  Ann replies.

  You know I have told you once to go to frank' s restaurant for food.

  She tells him.

- A yeah, eventually one day that we will eat outside.

  Ha ha.

  Robert says and laughs at her because they always eat out.

- O come on now.

  I think tony the Italian plays piano there, you will like it.

  She says.

- It will be done Ann, it will be done.

  Robert replies.

  Just a moment to choose a date in my calendar.

  He says.

  He puts out of his drawer his agenda with the calendar and opens it very carefully.

  It has private pages.

  Name of everyday people not someone very important.

  Also names of girls.

  He may be a person that wants to do with money these that he couldn' t do before without them.

  This is the only drawer that is locked.

  Even though elsewhere he could leave money for a while without locking the drawer.

- Okay Robert we will talk later again.

  Ann says.

- Bay bay.

Robert says.

- Jenna you know, I have yried once to read a book.

  I have read it until the one hundred page.

  The wole book was consisted of trirty hundred and

  The whole story was in the one hundred pages that I have read.

  Robert says.

- Why you are telling me that mister Morison?

  Jenna asks.

- Because you have to deal life like a small pocket book that has the necessary thing to give you and also advises and tips.

  And no as a big encyclopedia that you have to spend hours so to find something.

  You don't have to make the life as a hamburger, with many tastes on it.

  Because you will lose the real taste of life.

  I had this book since I was a kid.

  That' s why I know what someone doesn't think when I speak to him.

- You know I have observed that.

  It' s more clever to know what other can' t think so you will be always a step forward.

  Jenna says.

- I am happy we agree.

  Well, you came in and I relax.

  It is rarely to speak to someone and feel relaxed.

  You know many people want to talk to you just to show you something that they aren't or something that they think that it's right.

  This is very boring.

  Jim cartal is knocking again.

- Yes.

  Jim opens the door.

- Ok Jenna thank you for the co operation.

Robert says.

- Me too sir.

Jenna says and goes.

Jim is getting in and looking Jenna from behind.

- Lucky president.

Jim says and laughs.

- Speak of the devil.

Robert says referring that most of the people talk for a specific reason.

- What?

Jim says.

- Something that bothers me.

Jim says.

- Tell me what is it that you want?

Robert tells jim.

- Well, I found that some plans of our gadgets are stolen.

Jim says.

- How are you so sure?

Robert asks him.

- Well I found the photocopies of the plans in Martin' s bookshop.

Jim says.

- I used to leave there some plans so to share the plans to the department.

Don' t worry.

Robert says.

- A, so many years in this company I have never learned that.

Jim replies.

- Okay, every day is there a motivation.

Robert says.

- Yes I have learned something again.

  Jim says.

- Well I was looking a new idea, for cutting woods.

  I have brought the plan with me.

  Jim says.

  Jim puts the plan in the big office of Robert.

- Well I can see now here that you have written that we will use less iron than ususal.

  How reliable can this gadget be without iron.

  A gadget that is created to cut wood.

  Robert says.

- Well I don' t know, Kevin approved that.

  Jim says.

- Are you accusing my son?

  He says.

- He is in the testing department rob.

  I didn't accuse him.

  Jim replies.

- Get out now and let me think. Leave the plan here.

  Robert says.

  This is one of the very few times that Robert gets upset.

  At five o' clock he calls Jim again.

- Jim I saw the plan, well I believe that my son is right.

  He has redused the amount of iron in the position that is the button, instead of iron he put plastic.

  He has reduced the cost, because of that and because of other mistakes too, I fire you Jim.

  It is your fault.

  Go to Max to take your money.

- But, but.

Jim says.

- Go.

Robert says.

When jim gets out of robert' s office he meets sean.

He saw him upset.

- Ha ha, did he clean you?

He tells him.

Jim looks at him, doesn' t talk and goes.

Scene

Afternoon at six o' clock he is on the way to home.

In a spot that he likes to stand for a while, he doesn' t feel good.

He almost faint, but he manages to stand and go towards to a seat.

- I know, I know that I have a few days left.

He whispers.

I sold the home; I don't have anything now to cheer up myself.

After a few minutes of relaxing Robert gets up and goes at home.

He likes walking.

He likes the smell of his area; he likes to breathe the smell of foods that comes straight to his nose.

After a quarter he gets in his home.

Ann is sleeping.

Alan is not there.

Kevin is in a friend.

Liza is steel at hospital.

Robert sees the couch in the living room.

He must not seat there, this is ann' s rule.

He seats in a arm chair besides.

He sleeps there.

The next morning.

He gets up at nine o' clock.

This day wants to sleep more in the house he may want to stay more in this chair in living room, he may wants to has the smell of his home on his body.

After a few minutes he receives a phone call.

George calls Robert, Newman is next to George.

He changes his voice.

- Hello, old man.

  I know that you sold the home.

  You did it without paying the hores that you had rented once.

  He tells gim.

- But, but, what are you talking about?

  Who are you?

  Robert says.

- Don't fooling with me man.

  You know damn well, what I am talking about.

  I am talking about the money that you own to me.

  There must be 30.000 dollars approximately.

  I want them back.

  He says.

  Robert starts grouching.

  George made a mistake; he tells the price that he pays for the house.

- Now it is double.

  When you have been calling the wores you have never payed.

  Now it is double the price, what about it.

  I know you… scam

- What are you telling him, no no.

  Newman says to George.

- I may know you too.

  Robert says.

- I have your agenda with the names of wores inside.

  Robert useued to call call girls at the home he has sold to Newman.

  He hadn' t had sex with them, he was embarrassed about himself and body.

  He had another habit only to see them playing with themselves.

  This house was his only secret.

  A secret that was to be well known secret after his death.

- A now I see, you mean mister moriso.

  He is dead, my son, I am his brother.

  Robert tells without hesitation.

  He has understood that this man is George.

- What?

  George says.

- But when?

George asks.

- Ooo, he passed away sadenly.

Robert says.

Scene

Meanwhile.

George doesn' t speak.

Newman is looking at George.

- I don't know, I realy don' t but, but he wasn' t ready to go.

He wanted to stay more in this earth.

He wanted to do more things.

Robert says.

He pretends that he is a little crazy influented by the death of Robert.

- But excuse me sir, your voice is like his.

George says.

- We were very close to each other. Even our voices were similar.

Robert says.

- What' s your name please?

George asks.

- My name? well, my name is Nicoalas Eastdose sir.

I have the name of my first father.

He died and for his honour I kept this name, even though my mother got married again.

- O I am very sorry sir.

Your history is very emotional.

I apologise for this fact and for this calling also.

You know I am in the army and there we have some rules.

The first is to be men enough so to face the consequences.

If is something that I can do to help you please tell me.

George says.

- Well thank you for you understanding. There isn' t something thank you very much..

Robert replies.

- Okay sir, bay bay, have a nice day.

George replies.

- But what did he told you?

Newman asks George.

- He told me that Robert morison is dead.

George replies.

- What?

And what are you going to do?

We are losing now.

Louks will kill me.

Newman tells.

- My brother too.

You know that my brother wants to be in the business.

The only thing that he is doing now is to steel the photocopies of morison from Martin' s bookshop.

But morison used to leave there half of the plans for the gadgets and my brother that pays Martin to give him the plans is not been helped enough because of this that morison does.

He does it on purpose.

George says.

- He wants 15.000 more to do something more, but he can not take a loan because banks don' t trust him.

George continues.

- We have to think what to do.

  Newman says.

- We can threaten his family.

  George says.

- We, we don't' t have receipts.

  We only have his agenda, one agenda with names.

  Names can not give us hopes.

  Newman says.

- Shit, he has the contract too.

  Neman continues.

- What contract?

  George asks.

- You are mad?

  The contract for that house he sold you.

  Newman says.

- O, you said the magic word.

  The house he sold me.

  We can take advantage of that.

  George says.

- How?

  You don't have the keys yet.

  Newman says.

- There is no need to find the keys, but we have to find the wores.

  We will take them there and take them video that they admit that they got into this house for Robert morison.

  Geroge says.

- That' s agood idea.

  Ha ha.

Newman says.

-   Open the agenda.

    Newman says to George.

-   Well let phone to this girl here.

    George says.

-   I will speak to her.

    Newman says.

-   The number is wrong.

    He says.

-   Call another.

    George tells him.

-   Again wrong number.

    Newaman says.

    Newman calls other twelve.

    but all have wrong number.

    Robert has the habit to give them numbers that he have been made the contracts.

    After he used the girls he canceled the numbers.

    So now none of them has the numbers of the past.

    Meanwhile

    Robert is searching for his agenda.

-   O shit I lost it.

    Ha ha ha.

    He says and laughs.

-   He can not do anything against me.

    I remember the reason.

    Robert says.

Kevin comes to the home, ann is coming downstairs.

- Goodmorning dad.

  Kevin tells Robert.

- Goodmorning?

  This is noon my friend.

  Where have you been?

  He tells.

- I was expanding my affairs list.

  He replies.

- And now I will expand my body in the bed, excuse me.

  He continues.

- And what about the job? Who is going to test the gadgets? Me? E?

  Robert tells him.

- Every day consists job, tomorrow I will come.

  Kevin says.

- In the end of the month I will pay them all, I have the money and I have more.

  But each of on in the company will be paid for the hours that he worked and for the other hours that he hasn' t worked mister.

  Robert says and gets up from the armchair.

  He has sweated a little.

- Goodmorning ann.

  He says.

- Goodmorning,

  She says.

- Do you want orange juice?

  She asks him.

- Can you or you serve me or you have to see it in cook book? Ha ha ha.

  Robert tells him and laughs.

- O came on.

  She says.

- Why haven' t you divorced me, I didn' t want but since we have time now, this morning I would like to know.

  She tells him.

- Because our marriage was a deal.

  Don' t you remember?

  He replies.

The same day, at evening Robert had booked a table for to to a restaurant.

He took ann there to dance and to remember the years that passed.

After the dance the couple goes at home, but Robert when ann falls asleep, he leaves.

He travels to England with a night flight.

Robert starts to play with the people that hurt him.
He plays as in a game.
He likes monopoly and desides to treat the people as peons.
He is in England now in a small poor hotel in a little room without a very nice view.
He is not interested for luxury any more.
He has a plan on a table in front of him.
- Well, well, well, with whom I shall begin.

  He sais.

  He is not willing to take revenge from each one either to make them destroy each other, he is willing to confuse them so to make the regret or become better people.

  He hasn' t a specific plan for each he is willing to play as the game leads and as he wants too.

- The first is to make my family better.

  Firstly Ann, afterwards Alan and then Kevin.

He sais.

He is looking his self at the round mirror.

He is making a life briefing.

Sitting in his chair and having his hand on the desk holding his head.

The breeze is coming through the open window.

He is missing this sense of freedom and breeze of his village.

He starts drawing something on the paper, he may feels like child again.

Alone but not feeling loneliness.

He may feels the power of choice, that has now.

The choice that he made leaving everything behind him and out of his new world that he made.

The same time his family s at job, this is the first time that his wife was at the company after he established that since 1977.

Not because he didn't' t like to involve his wife to financial things and business but because she didn't' t want to visit him there.

They speak with max, mark and Robbie in a while Jim Cartal comes in the conference room.

They gathered there and wondering what happened to Robert.

Mark stars speaking.

- I am afraid of Robert' health.

He hasn' t done examinations for long.

He says.

Meanwhile

Scene

Robert is in his room alone as always.

Robert always wanted to make a trip abroad he had never done even if he used to have a boat.

He couldn' t have the happiness of a poor man that could go at least a small walk and seems to him as a big trip.

Robert couldn' t go the big travels that some were dreaming and he was feeling that he was living in a dead end.

The boat was usually in the dock and sometimes the latest years only Alan was taking that.

Now that he managed to do the trip, he will not be able for long to tell himself that he did it.

He is dying.

Scene

He has learned everything about everybody.

He makes a call.

- Hello.

Sais carol.

He called George the neighbor firstly because he made him the biggest harm.

- Hello madame.

He sais with a little heavy voice like he has a problem because of smoking, even though he had never smoked.

He pretends.

- I am mister Eastdose.

  He always liked east.

- I am calling for the dog that your husbandl killed yesterday.

  Is your husband a big man?

  You know that dog was the only joy that I had in my life and for it I was the only joy too.

  He did it with his car.

  He starts pretending that he is crying.

- Oh yes, George is my husband, what a pity, but where, how?

  I am carol his wife.

  To tell you the truth, I overheared him once saying " I passesd very closed to this damn dog".

  Carol sais.

- What difference does it make my kind lady.

  I believe by your voice that you love animals.

- Ooo, that is sure mister, excuse me, your name is...

  Carol replies.

- Eastdose.

  Robert sais.

- You know it was cost 60.000 I had bought it from an organation that helps animals and because it was the last dog of that specific kind it was very expensive, it had to be in a very good environment, to get feed very well and to be raised with love.

  I had taken recently my pension and because I have work many years I had made a fortune.

  But I am alone, I hadn' t made family because my illness, I am phimatic.

  The only joy and happiness was this animal.

  Robert sais.

- Ooo your poor man, you know I am e teacher in school for blind kids and even they are blind they all love animals even thy can not see the animals approache them, I am learning the kids to love animals..

  What can I do to help you.

  Carols tells him.

- Well I have a nephew that is blind and loves animals, but because there is a chance for him to see again he needs money to go abroad for operation.

  He liked this puppy, imagine that every time puppy was seeing him he was licking him.

  My nephew is nine years old and the puppy was one year old.

  They loved each other.

  It is more important to me to give 60.000 to my nephew for the operation than buying him a puppy.

  He sais.

- Oh but of course.

  She sais.

- Well my husband is at the army and even he thinks I am stupid I know that somewhere she has old golden coins.

  That he has made was a crime.

  Carol sais without asking details of the fact.

  Robert had persuaded.

- I will find them and give them to you.

  I heard him one day that he was telling that they don' t worth, but I believe they worth that' s why he store them.

  Just a moment sir to find them.

  Robert is waiting in the line.

He is hearing her walking in the wooden old floor.

After a while Carol is coming back.

He is hearing that she is walking fast.

- Mister eastdose, are you in the line?

She is saying with her sweet and a bit tired voice.

- Yes madam I am here.

Robert replies.

- I found them.

She sais.

- How can I give them to you?

I don' t know how much money they are.

She says.

- Well never mind, they are golden?

Robert asks her.

- Well yes, mister Eastdose.

She replies.

- Well I don't want you to believe that I do it for the money but for a good reason.

Robert sais.

- Could you tell me in where these coins are inside?

Robert asks.

- In a wooden box.

Carol sais.

- Is it heavy?

He asks her.

- Yes a lot.

She says.

- Can you lift it?

  He asks her.

- No I am dragging it.

  She sais.

- Which is its depth?

  She asks her.

- I can' t tell, its locked.

  She replies.

- You can check from outside.

  He replies.

- O yes you are right.

  What a fool I am.

  She sais.

- Just a moment please.

  I' ll bring a ruler.

- Well, this is 50 centimeters mister Eastdose.

  She says.

- Okay misses Carol.

  He says.

Robert by asking these things he realized that there is a lot of money.

- Well I will send a young guy there to collect them.

  Could you tell me your address please?

  Robert sais.

He pretends that he doesn't know.

Scene

Robert is pretending that he is writing the address.

- Ok madam, thank you very much, I will send you a gift for your kind movement, I will never forget you.

Robert says.

- O what are you talking about, the destiny played a bad game to you and I can not understand why my husband didn't tell me something.

Carol says.

- Bay bay misses carol

Robert is calling bob.

- Ey, bob…

He says.

- Don' t tell my name.

He says continuing to speak as before.

He forgot that he was talking like having problem and that he was pretending.

- What, who is it?

Bob says.

Robert speaks again with his real voice.

- It's me, Robert Morison.

He says.

- Ooo, mister…

Bob says avoiding the last minute to say the surname of Robert.

- Where are you now?

Robert asks.

- A just a moment my friend, just a moment because I am in a meeting in job.

Bob is in the conference room with family of Robert and some of the other colleges of him.

Scene

He is going outside the room.

- I am in the first floor, in the conference room.

  He sais.

Robert had decided to make the conference room in the lowest floor just in case of earthquake.

His thought was to make that in order if there was an earthquake during a meeting at least most of the people would leave immediately.

- Well. First of all I want you to know that I am fine.

  Also that I am very close to you all.

He is lying to protect himself.

- I want you to make something for me.

  All this years I have never told you to do something for me and as I can understand you may complain for that.

  Well now is your turn.

  Robert says.

- Well, it would be my pleasure as far as it concerns the job.

  Bob replies.

- Well it is nothing about the job.

  It is something personal.

Robert says.

- Personal?

Bob replies surprised.

- Yes personal, I want you to kill somebody.

Robert says.

- To kill somebody?

But what…

What are you talking about?

Robert stars laughing.

Scene

- Ha ha ha.

I have never laughed such this way before, ha ha.

Robert says.

- I am joking.

He continuous.

Meanwhile Robert is seeing a man from his window jogging in the street.

In the beginning he thoughts he was familiar to him.

- Mister Morison…

Bob whispers.

Robert was stuck looking outside.

- Mister morison.

Bob says again a little bit louder.

- Yes, yes, I am here.

Speak louder bob.

- You told me not to tell your name and I remind you that I am near the conference room, in the same floor with it.

Bob says.

- Ok, you are right.

  Robert replies.

- Well, I want you to do something that has nothing to do with the company.

  But with some people.

  You have to see it as assignment.

  Nobody has to learn about this assignment.

  Robert says.

- Will I be in dangerous?

  Bob asks.

- No not at all.

  Robert replies.

- I must not tell it to anyone?

  My girlfriend, friends, your relatives?

  Bob asks.

- I don' t have friends only people that I know and they know me too.

  That' s why I want you not to tell to anybody.

  Robert replies.

- Ok.

  What I have to do?

  Bob says.

- You have to go to my neighbors to take something.

  Go with a car or bike.

  You may not be able to lift it.

  Robert sais.

- You will find misses Carol tell her that you are...

  Robert is thinking.

- My assistant because I am unable.

  Robert tell him.

- But you have to move fast, go now.

  Robert tells him.

- After you take that she will give, transfer it to the old warehouse of the company, not in the new one.

  I have there some old computers.

  The screens of some are broken, put the box in one of the screens.

  It must t feats.

- Bay for now.

  Robert tells bob.

- Ok, bay mister...oops.

  Bob says and catches his mouth.

  Bob enters the conference room.

- Sorry but I have to go, something came up.

  He says.

- But we are looking for a solution here bob.

  Jim Cartal tells him.

- The boss of our company is missing.

  Jim continues.

- Maybe because you were used to call him rob.

  Bob tells him.

- Sorry I have to go.

  Bob tells looking everybody and leaves the building.

- The boss is not here and he does everything he wants.

  When rob, e Robert comes back I will notify him.

  scene

Bob is going to parking of the company and takes his car.

Jim cartal is seeing him from the window of the conference room.

He is nodding his head.

He is out of fuel.

- Shit.

The time is running against him and he knows that.

He pusses the car until the next fuel shop.

Afterwards he drives fast to misses Carol.

Scene

In a few minutes he arrives at her home.

He goes to her home's door.

He rings the bell.

Scene

Carol opens.

- Hello young boy.

Carol sais.

- Have you came for the coins?

Carol asks bob.

Robert had never mentioned to bob about the coins.

He had only told him about the box.

- Eee, hello, yes madam.

For the coins.

Mister Morison sent me.

Bob replies.

He betrayed Robert when he learns that money are in the box.

Bob makes a mistake by saying the name Morison.

Carol may not heared the name that bob told, but bob isn' t sure about that.

- O okay.

Carol says.

Carol has already get the box out of the home, Bob saw it, but...

- Just a moment to bring you the box, I have that for cleaning; my husband wants to clean it so to shine.

Carol goes in the home and brings another box, same with the other one.

She pretends that it is heavy.

She pretends that she is breathing difficult while she is in the home.

Bob is hearing from outside and seems happy he smiles and claps his hands once.

She brings the box.

Bob now takes his serious style.

- I am weak, you know.

Carol says.

- Here is you box.

She says.

Bob takes it.

It seems not to heavy for him.

- Okay madam, thank you very much, I shall take it now.

Bay bay.

He tells her.

Scene

He takes the box and goes to his car.

Carol watches him.

He turns his head back, he sees her, she say to him bay bay nodding her hand.

He smiles to her.

He gets in his car.

He watches her from the central mirror.

She is looking at him.

He goes.

She put her hand in her chin and thinking.

Scene

Bob is going to an empty alley; he finds a street that nobody passes at the moment.

It happened to be behind carol's home.

bob made a cyrcle.

He opens the box that has next to him to the seat.

-   Oh, she fooled me.

He sais.

The box is full of napkins and towels.

Scene

The same time carol is going to bring back the other box with the coins.

She sees that the box is missing.

Bob walk fast towards the home and took the box with the coins.

He had time to write a note too.

" thank you for the help".

- Ooo, they robbed me they robbed me.

  Carol is shouting.

Scene

The same time George arrives at home.

- Why are you shouting you crazy woman?

  He asks her angry.

  She doesn' t talk.

- Speak.

  George tells her.

- Somebody stole the box with coins.

  She tells him.

- What?

  He tells.

- They entrapped me.

  She says.

- Who?

  Someone Morison.

  She says.

- Oh you damn old woman.

  You gave him the coins.

He tells her and he lifts his hand to hit her.

He hit her and pushed her inside the home.

The voice of Carol that is screaming stops after a few seconds.

Scene

Bob is now in the car and goes somewhere far.

- O yeah, that' s why Morison had never trust me, but now I made him believe that he was right without knowing that of course.

Ha ha ha.

He says laughing.

Robert is seeing his watch.

The time passed.

He calls bob.

- Yes, yes mister Morison.

Bob says with his fake good voice to his boss.

- What about the job?

Robert asks him.

- E, okay mister Robert.

Bob sais.

- Where are you now?

Robert asks him.

- I am going to the warehouse.

Bob tells him.

Bob is driving through the street next to the see, not heading to the warehouse but somewhere else.

Robert is hearing the sea.

But he doesn' t saying something.

Because Robert doesn' t talk, bob start speaking.

- I am making a cyrcle in case someone has followed me.

Bob sais to save himself.

- Ok bob.

We will talk later.

Scene

Bob goes at his home.

scene

- Ok the case George is done.

Robert says.

He erases with a pen the name George.

He throws away the black peon.

- Now, as I can think, I shall deal with Max, Max hurt me to.

Robert sais.

He calls at the company.

Nobody answers.

Scene

The phone is ringing.

Everybody has left.

Scene

Max receives a phone call.

He is at his home.

He is making a plan for the expenses and income of the company.

He erases the expenses so that Robert doesn'ts know about them in order to earn the money and after Robert has to pay more because of the increasing of fees, apart from the fact that he takes the contracts of sales and changes the names on these, putting his so to collect the money on behalf the company.

- Yes, who is it?

He speaks as always with anxiety.

- Hello max, I am Robert.

Robert says.

- O hello mister Morison, but, but where are you?

Max says.

- Don' t worry I am close toy all, I can see you.

Robert tells in purpose.

- A, ok mister Morison I only want to know if are fine and I want to inform you that I am protecting the company and your profit too.

Max says.

- Ok Max Viewing I know that, I am fine.

Robert says.

- Well I don' t intend to come back soon.

I has left an envelope in my office that I need it.

It' s a green envelope that has a label wrights mister Viewing.

You have to give it to Mark.

Robert says.

- Ok, do you mine telling what this envelope consists?

  Max asks him.

- A, some examinations that I have done in the past, with my medical history too.

  Robert tells him.

- A ok. There is no problem.

  Max says.

- Thank you very much.

  Robert says.

- I knew I could rely on you.

  He continues.

Scene

It' s noon.

Max is packing his papers pus them in his suitcase and goes to the company.

Scene

He gets into the lift.

He goes to Robert' s office in the third floor.

He sees the envelope.

He takes it and goes to get in the lift again.

He is looking everywhere in the lobby of the company.

He is afraid of what he had done.

Before he left the building, suddenly he hears a voice.

- In the life you must have that you worth.

A voice familiar to him says.

Max looks back while he is towards the main door of the company, without turning back.

After one second he turns back.

The voice is from jack.

Max is seeing jack and stands as a statue.

Jack has changed.

He is not the ugly, not good looking man.

He has shaved his beard and he has done his hair.

Jack is steele an old man, but now he is well looking.

Scene

- Ooo, what a change. But what do you mean?

Max tells him.

- Robert always was laughing at me.

Now he may be dead, he may suicide, because of depth.

As far as I could understand by the people who were coming in here, the company was going good.

He used to say that I stink, even if he thoughts I couldn't' t hear him.

all these years I was pretending someone else.

I am not so old, my hands and feet are working well as far.

I want to destroy him.

Jack says.

- What? You want to destroy him because he used to tell that you stink?

Are you crazy?

Max sais.

97

- Robert had files for each of us.

  Even in this envelope he could put something bad for you.

  Jack says.

  Max looks the envelope.

- You are insane.

  These are some examinations.

  Max says.

- Are you sure?

  That's what he told you.

- Nonsense.

  Max says.

- Open it.

  Jack says.

- O come on man give me a break.

  Max tells him and preparing to go us he turns his back to jack.

- But what were you 've been doing here?

  max asks jack.

- This is the time I usually waters the plants.

  Jack says.

- Ok. Buy buy.

  Max says.

- But tell me, will we co operate?

  Jack asks him.

- I will think of it.

  Max tells him while he is walking to the door.

  He gets out.

  scene

- You crazy ha ha ha.

  Max whispers.

  He is seeing the green envelope.

  He hesitate a little to walk and he focus the envelope.

  But he keeps walking.

  Max is calling mark.

- Mark, hello, sorry to disturb you.

  He says.

  Mark is leaving from a pub.

, He is walking.

- Hello, never mind, I am on the road to home.

  What's up?

- I have an envelope that mister Morison told me to give you.

  Max says.

- Morison, but when did you see him.

  Mark asks him.

- I didn't see him.

  He called me.

  Max says.

- A okay, well, can you come to Jey's pub?

  I will wait for you outside.

  Mark says.

- Jey's pub?

  You know I don't go to pubs often.

  Where is it?

  Max says.

- It's four quarters ahead of the home of Morison.

Mark tells him.

- A okay, I have passed once from there.

I am coming.

Scene

Max goes to his car.

He sees a newspaper on the road.

Scene

He sees the column of goran hoffway, " the fact of 24 hours ", a big title.

Her name was sue, only 22 years old so many years to come but in a few minutes only she left dead.

Goran's column is the lovely of Robert.

The newspaper of the previous week that Goran has his column was left by Robert next to the green envelope on her desk.

He reads the title and goes.

He gets his car from the parking.

Turns on the radio that plays an old song and starts driving.

The dark is coming slowly bad steady.

In a few minutes it will be all over the city.

Only a few people are out in the neighbourgh that is mark now.

Most of the people are relaxing at their homes.

In a half an hour Max gets to Mark.

He goes by his car next to Mark.

Max during he is driving puts out of the window the envelope before he stops the car.

Scene

- Ey Max get off the car to buy you a drink.

    Mark tells him while he is standing next to Max' s car.

- O you know I have to go at home, my wife is waiting for me, she wants to go to-gether to a eat out.

    He says.

- O, shit, you have to buy her food and eat with her, and she has to make sex with you.

    I won' t never married man, I won' t never do this mistake.

    I will continue picking a girl one night and as long as it last.

    Mark says.

- Ok, mark you are right, but what are you going to do when you will not be able to pick and no one girl would pick you?

    Max says to him.

- Well I have to think of that, but Intend to be good looking enough so to avoid this problem.

    Mark replies.

- Take this envelope Mark.

    Max tells.

- Ok, thank you.

    Mark says.

- It has his medical history as he told me.

    Max says.

We have to make elections for the leadership of the company, as you know Robert hadn't never said that his children are after him in the leadership.

In the rules of the company he has written that we have to make elections.

- I imagine that this is the medical history.

He probably wants to make examinations.

I believe that is very soon to do it.

Why don't wait a few days, he may returns.

Bay bay.

Mark says.

- See you soon.

Max replies with anger.

Scene

Robert calls mark.

- Hello.

Mark says.

- Hello mark.

Robert says.

- Ooo Robert where are you?

How is your daughter?

Mark says.

- She is better now.

Robert says.

Robert hasn' t spoken with his family yet.

- Has max given you an envelope?

Robert tells mark.

- Yes Robert, he has.

Mark says.

- Okay, I want you to give to Robbie.

  Tomorrow morning.

  Robert tells him.

- Okay, but, Robert when are you going to come?

  You know max told me earlier that we have to make elections for the leadership.

  I am not in the members of the company, I don' t have problem with the elections, also I don't want the leadership.

  But he told me something that I didn't know, none of your children are your first choice for the leadership.

  Why is that?

  Mark says.

- I don't know, but I don't trust them, that's why.

  They haven't worked like me and they can not understand how I earn money, how I earned, because now the company isn't going so good.

  Robert says.

- Okay I agree with you, but you know, maybe they are people in the company that have benefits from the elections.

  Mark says.

- What do you mean?

  Robert says.

- Come on Robert.

  Mark says.

- Don't you have understood anything?

  Mark says.

- Well, some things yeah, that's why I want to give this envelope to Robbie.

  It's about a person that I have a lot of doubts that he is interested in the company and me too.

  Robert says.

- What do you mean?

    Mark says.

- Tell me first mark.

    Robert tells him.

- Well I mean Max.

    Mark says.

- That envelope refers to him Mark.

    I have collected some clues that show that max is guilty of some things.

    Robert says.

- I may not come back.

    He continues.

    He coughs.

- Robert, Robert, you are not so good, do not get tired my friend.

    I will send you a medicine and a form to fulfill.

    Mark says.

- Ok Mark, I have to hung up now.

    Robert says.

scene

He seats on a chair and start sweating.

He sleeps, but it seems as he fainted.

There is no room service in this hotel, he is alone.

Scene

Mark is going at his office.

He opens his computer and writes a form.

He writes a form that robert gives the company to Mark because of health problem.

The next day in morning.

After six days

Robert had done everything that he likes and had had time to do.

Robert is relaxed.

He hadn' t give any sign of life to nobody again.

He tries to call at his home.

The line is busy.

Scene

Liza is at home.

She seats in her bed.

She doesn't go at work.

Liza is at her room.

He is calling Vick.

- Hello Vick.

  I am Liza.

  How are you?

  She says.

- Hello, who is it?

  He says as if he hasn' t waken up yet.

- Liza, do you remember that we have said to meet each other to co operate?

Liza says.

- Ooo, I remember something, but can I call you back in a minute?

Vick tells her.

- O that' s okay.

She says.

- Okay, bitch?

He says like whispering, so Liza didn't hear the "bitch".

- Mmm, what he said?

Never mind.

Liza says.

Vick was sleeping with two starlets.

One blond and one brunette.

These two women are covered by the sheet.

Only their hairs are shown.

- Ooo, who was that now?

Vick says and continues sleeping.

After a few hours passed Liza is calling again Vick because he didn't call her.

- Yes, excuse me Vick, I have called you earlier.

Liza says.

- Oo, yeah, have I told you something wrong?

Vick says with anxiety.

He was drunk, and has taken drugs too.

- Well, no never mind.

She says, thinking to tell him about the bitch but she doesn't eventually.

- I am calling to arrange an appointment.

She tells.

- You have told me a week ago that you could today.

She continues.

- O, yeah, but something came up and we have to meet each other tomorrow.

  He says.

- A, okay, I don't have problem with that.

  Liza says.

- Okay, bay.

  He says to her.

- Bay bay, a will you call me?

  She asks, but he had already hung up.

- He didn't call me back later, I hope he will tomorrow.

  She says.

  She grapes her pillow and puts it among her legs.

  She squeezes it.

- Ooo, I have to wait another one day.

  She says.

  scene

  Vick gets of the bed.

- Ha ha ha.

  I will earn money from that bitch.

  He says.

- How foolish people there are out there.

  He says looking out of his window pulling a little bit the courtin.

- They believe in something that can last a few days and they don' t give attention in the permanent.

  He opens his fridge and takes a beer.

  He opens it and drinks.

Scene

Meanwhile.

Alan is still traveling with the boat.

Kevin calls him.

- Ey Alan where are you?

    He says.

- Man man I am not intending to come back.

    I have my freedom here.

    I am alone without commitments and free of all.

    He replies.

- Ooo man why didn' t you tell me to join you?

    Kevin says.

- Because you are the son of dad.

    You are doing all the things with plan.

    Be free for a while.

    I don' t have problem for you to come and join me, but if I have told you, you would have to think of that very much, so much that I would leave again alone.

    I am in caribean sea.

    Afterwards I don' t know.

    That' s life my brother.

    Well I have to go now, I will make surf, I can see gilrs in the beach I am going to talk to all.

    Bay.

    Alan says.

- You crazy ha ha ha.

    Kavein says.

Scene

Meanwhile.

Robert is drawing and writing in his plan on the table.

He has ordered food.

After a while he feels bored.

- Well, Robert, let's go for a walk.

He says.

He gets up of the table, but he starts sweating.

He seats down again.

- Oh, my days are few.

Let's have some fun.

As much as I can.

He tells with difficulty.

He is trying to get up.

He eventually made it.

Bat a few seconds after he did it, he falls to the floor.

He wakes up in the evening.

He thinks.

- Let the day to pass.

He says.

He is not In a mood to do something.

Kevin calls him.

- Ey dad, where are you?

He tells him.

- I have met a girl yesterday, and I want you to tell me your opinion.

She lives in another state.

You think it' s worth to go there?

- Man has to belike the road.

  He has to go everywhere.

  Robert says.

- And if the road doesn' t go somewhere?

  Kevin asks.

- Then you have to make your own road.

  Robert replies.

- Where did you meet her?

  Robert says.

- Well I have'n t met her yet, a friend of mine gave me her phone and we have spoken.

  That' s all.

  He says.

- Well my son, I 'd prefer to advise you when I am there rather doing this from here I am.

  The best thing in this occasion is to contact her and have a date.

  You can invite her for a drink or for food.

  Go to frank restaurant in which you can listen to very nice music.

- I would prefer to seat as a family in the couch in living room.

  I don' t care if we ruin the silk or something like that, I will be glad to do it some day, because we will see that we are capable of that, instead of being unable for everything.

  Robert says.

- I understood your point dad.

  I wish you to come soon.

  Kevin replies.

- O now she is calling me dad I have second line.

  Kevin says happy.

- Okay my son I wish you luck bay bay.

  Robert says.

- Bay bay, I love you dad.

  Kevin replies.

The next morning liza is calling vick.

- Hello Vick, I am liza.

  She says.

- A, okay liza come to meet me to jo' s motel.

  He says.

- When?

  She replies.

- Now, girl, now.

  He replies.

  She start dressing fast, she put a little make up and go downstairs.

Scene

Ann sees her.

- E, liza where are you going?

  Ann says.

- To meet the dream.

  Lizaa replies.

Scene

Liza takes the car and spinning the tires she leaves.

Tom sees her while he returns from the job.

He says goodmorning but he doesn' t get an answer.

He is left with his hand up an as he had node to liza.

- Very strange behavior.

Rich men.

Is logical.

He says and goes at home.

- Mom, mom?

But where is she?

- She is at school, she will work more today.

George says sadenly.

- A, you scared my man.

Tom says.

- Okay I am going to sleep for a while I almost shit myself again yesterday, now I want to relax and to forget it.

Tom says.

Scene

Meanwhile liza is getting to the hotel.

She parks outside the door of the hotel.

She gets out and waits.

- Aaa, will someone come to park my car?

She shouts.

- Doll, come up here, this is not the Hilton.

In the first floor.

Vick says.

- A, okay.

She locks the car..

She is angry.

- You pathetic loosers.

You will never see me here again.

She refers to the hotel, she gets in.

She goes to the lift.

It's out of order.

- Shit, I have to go with stairs.

She says.

She eventually goes to the first floor.

One room's door is open.

- Come in.

Vick says.

He understood that liza got to the floor.

Scene

Vick is not alone.

He is seating in the couch and opposite him another other man is seating in another couch too.

The other man is called Buss Douglas.

A tall black hear guy, with a little beard round his lipas and chin.

A little fat,

He wears black cloths and tie with white shirt.

When liza got into the room both of the gentlemen got up.

- Hello liza.

Vick says.

- Hello.

She replies.

- This is mister Douglas.

  A very good friend.

- Nice to meet you sir.

  Liza says.

  Douglas takes her hand gently and kiss it.

- Nice to meet you too.

  He says.

  Liza and douglas are looking each other.

  But douglas was start this.

- Well have a seat liza.

  You too Buss.

  Vick says.

- Well, liza.

  Mister douglas is a manager like me, but he is specialist in another job.

  We intend to help you.

- As if I want to help myself and you too?

  Liza says.

- O yeah, that's what I would say.

  Vick says.

- Ha ha.

  He laugs and douglas too, bat a bit less than vick.

  He pretends the serious guy of the ompany.

- My dad used to tell that to me often.

  Liza says.

- Okay liza, had your dad agreed with your choice to deal with showbiz?

  Vick asks.

- Well my dad doesn't agree with almost anything.

She says.

- Ha ha.

  Vick laughs.

- If you want you tell me what is your dad's professional?

  Vick asks liza.

- He has a company, a big company, he makes inventions and gadgets.

  She replies.

- A fine fine.

  Vick says.

- Well. Mister Douglas will be your personal agent, he will arrange your jobs, to whom you will talk to and your clients.

  Vick says.

- My clients?

  Liza asks.

- Yes you will have clients.

  Vick says.

- You mean companies that I will advertise their products?

  Liza asks.

- Something like this.

  You will work and for persons too.

  You will be their escort.

  I want to be honest with you.

  Vick says.

- What do you mean by that?

  Liza asks.

- You have to go to hotels in order to welcome people.

  Vick says.

- What, but I have been prepearing my voice and body for something big.

Liza says.

- Well liza, don' t worry.

    You did very well.

    Your effort will be awarded.

    Vick says.

- Yes liza listen to vick, he is a man of the business.

    He doesn' t say something wrong.

    Douglas says.

- Liza Douglas is right, if you want to get involed with this form of bussines, modeling, photo shooting, sing, you have to begin from the lower step.

    Vick says.

- Okay, I understood, I accept this, but after this, what is next?

    Liza says.

    Vick is going to speak.

    Liza is catching her head.

- I feel dizzy.

    She says.

- Can I go to bathroom?

    She says.

- Yes of coure.

    Vick sais and gets up to saw her the bathroom.

    Liza is going fast to the bathroom.

    She vomits.

Meanwhile the two men are discussing.

Scene

- Well man, this girl is very beautiful.

Douglas says to vick.

- Yes..

Vick says.

They are close to each other bending a little toward to speak like whispering.

Liza is making noise while she opens the door of the bathroom.

- She is coming.

Vick says.

The two men seat back in normal place so to liza could not understand that the were talking about her.

- Sorry but I haven' t felt very good before.

She says.

- O no don' t apologise.

Douglas says.

- Have a seat.

He says.

- O sorry, I have to leave.

She replies.

- I am not very well.

She continues.

The two men get up.

- Ok liza we will keep in touch.

Vick says.

- I had your contract here but if you don' t feel well, never mind you will sign it next time.

He says.

- Contract?

Liza says glad.

-   Yes.

    Vick says and he puts it out of his pocket.

-   E well, can I take that at home?

    She says.

-   A no, you should sign it now, in front of us.

    Vick says.

-   A well, I coud stay for a while.

    She says.

-   Ok, but if you ar not very well it is better for you to get rest.

    Douglas says.

-   No I feel better now.

    She says.

-   Ok, have a seat again.

    Douglas says.

-   Ha ha, I am seating all the day.

    Liza says and seats.

-   Can I read it first?

    She says.

-   E, okay, but it is nothing bad.

    Vick says.

    Vick gives the contract to Liza.

-   You can read it there is chance to sign something bad, we will not blackmail you, like the movies you see, we are professionals.

    Vick says.

    Liza is reads the contract.

-   Well there is nothing here about salary.

    She says.

-   Well, salary depends on the hours that you will work.

It's like you work in sales department.

You earn more if you sale more.

Douglas says.

- You will meet people, very important people.

  But firstly we have to test in many situations to see if you are the girl that we need and if you worth to do this job.

  If we see that you don't feet, we will suggest you something else.

  Douglas continues.

- Well, do you agree?

  He continues.

- Well, I suppose I don' t have another choice.

  Liza says.

- Ha ha.

  You have, you can stay at home and find another job.

  You are young and pretty the future is yours.

  Douglas says.

- I' d prefer to sign instead of living a life o misery.

  Liza says.

- Misery?

  Vick asks.

- What is the benefit of being rich if you don' t can use your money?

  I work at my dad' s company and I take salary.

  Don' t imagine that I live as I like.

  She says.

  Liza catches her stomach.

- Well I guess I have to leave.

  I am not feeling well.

  She says.

- Okay, as soon as there a job for you we will notify you.

  Vick says as he gets up to say goodbay to liza.

  Douglas gets up too.
- Okay, thanks, bay bay.

  Liza says and goes a little fast.
- Bay bay.

  The two men say.

Scene

Liza goeas at her car.

She barely faints before she gets in.

She grap the door of the car to avoid falling.

She gets in.
- Ooo, what do I have?

  She says with difficulty.

  She is dizzy again.
- O shit, I don' t want to believe it.

  I am pregnant?

  She says with anger.

  She goes to matt.

Scene

She rings his bell.

She doesn' t get an answer.

She insists.

Sadenly matt scares her from behind.

He closes her eyes.

- Oo you scared me.

She tells him angry.

- What happened doll?

He tells her.

- Oo.

She says but after she faints.

Matt takes her in his house.

- What happened again?

You want your dose?

He says because she can't listen to him.

He puts her to lye on the couch.

He goes to brings a glass of water.

Liza is a little better and wakes up.

- What happened liza?

He tells her.

- You don' t know?

E?

I think I am pregnant.

She tells.

- What? With whom?

Ha ha.

matt replies.

- With you.

Then You knew how to take advantage of me, now you don' t know with whom I am pregnant?

If my dad learns about this?

Liza says.

- Your dad won't learn about this and I remind you that you liked that then.

matt tells.

- Ooo, you ruined me.

Liza says as she gets up of the couch.

- What am I going to do now?

She continues.

- You will have your baby, every woman wants that.

Don't you?

Matt tells her.

- Yes, yes, but...

Liza says.

- But what.

Not with me? E?

Matt says.

- You are just a junky. How can I put you in my house and in my life?

She tells.

- From the door my love, from the door, ha ha.

Don't get panic.

We will find a solution.

Do you have money for abortion?

Matt says.

- Are you laughing at me?

Liza says.

I don't believe you.

- No my love, I don't.

Your old man has a personal doctor, hasn't he?

Every rich man has one.

He says.

- What are you talking about?

He will kill me if he finds it out.

I will born that baby and you will face the consequences.

Liza takes the glass of water and throw the water to matt.

- Aaaa, you bitch.

He says.

After that Liza leaves.

Scene

Meanwhile

jenna is at the company.

She is calling bob.

- Ey bob where are you?

She says.

- I don't intend to come back.

I won in lottery a big budget.

I am leaving abroad.

If you weren' t lebian I would have told you to join me.

He tells her.

- What?

How dare you?

Who told you that I am a lesbian?

She says.

- Ooo, come on, how a pretty girl like you never had an affair so many years in the company?

Either you are lesbian or you you have a disease.

I cannot explain that in other way.

Bob says.

- Ooo how double-faced are you?

That's why mister Morison never trusted you.

She says to him.

- Never?

I doubt on that Jenna.

But I won't let you know how and when.

Well I want you to inform the others that I won't come back.

Jim Cartal passes close to Jenna.

She nodes to him to stop.

Jim approaches.

Jenna covers the microphone with her hand.

- It is bob, he tells that he won't come to job, he won in lottery.

Jenna tells Jim.

- Okay bob as you want, but please inform mister Morison.

I will say that to Robert if he calls me.

I am calling him but I cannot reach him.

Robert had changed his number.

Robert thinks to call at the company at Jim.

But instead he thinks it again and calls bob first.

Robert seats in the the couch.
He brings in his mind the past.
Images of other times.
- I remember that we didn' t seat in the couch in the living room, ann always used to say that this couch is for specific times.

What if you have something and you are afraid of use it just in case you damage it.

You may wait for a specific moment to come and this time would never come.

Meanwhile

Newman is calling George..

- Hello, george, loukas called me.

  He says.

- And what about him?

  george says.

- He wants the money man, he wants them.

  Have you threatened morison?

  Newman asks him with anger.

- I 've called him, but, but.

  You remember.

  He told me that he knows me man and after he told me that he wasn' t Robert but his brother.

  Ooo I am scared.

  he entrapped me man, he took me the money.

  George says and starts crying.

- O yeah I forgot it, then threaten him, Estdose. I am at the seventh street now, I am looking for an old friend to get rid of this old man, the brother of morison. What money?

  I don' t want you mean the coins?

  O shit, I will kill you man, I swear to god, I will.

  You made me your enemy.

  Newman says.

- But, but wait, I have threatened him and after he took me the money.

  George replies.

- O you bastard, I have told you to give me that box to keep the coins safe.

Your silly wife must had given him the coins.

Now what?

We are a step back and he is a step forward.

Where are you now, I am coming to find a solution, ooo, help, ooo.

He says.

The sound of a car hitting someone is hearing.

- Michael, where tha fuck are you man?

George says.

George is going to find Newman.

He found him lying in the street.

He is dead.

Many people are around him.

George asks someone.

He tells him that he saw a green car with spot for flag in the fender.

This car belongs to loukas he thinks.

He killed him.

He reads in goran' s column that loukas retired because he couldn' t find money for the elections and his campaign.

- O shit.

He says.

- Now is my turn.

He says.

He leaves he is looking everywhere.

He thinks that somebody is looking him from a roof.

He always looking high.

He falls in a bus.

George is killed too.

Scene

Meanwhile

Alan is back, he doesn' t know that his dad has left.

He goes and writhes to his block his exoiriences and what he did the days that he wasn' t home.

Every day he used to write at this block afterwards he hide it in the crypt under his bed.

" I killed sue. "

He writes and afterwards he goes to living room.

Kevin and allan go to seat in the couch that never no one seat there except of birthdays that taken place there very rarely because Robert was a little unsocial and his family odd.

Kevin says to Alan that their father left.

Meanwhile.

Liza is with vick.

They are in the hippodromes.

They were together the night before.

- Well, I have arranged you a job for today.

Vick says.

- O, okay.

What about it?

She asks.

- It' s about modeling.

Vick replies.

- A nice, I am interested. Oh, I have a pain in stomach again, can we leave?

She says, she doesn' t feel well.

- Okay, just a moment stay here I will bring the car.

He tells her.

Vick brings the car, it is an old camaro.

it has a bullet hole in the door of driver.

Vick had avoided arrest once.

Liza doesn' t see the hole.

She gets in.

She pains.

- Do you want to get you in a doctor?

He tells her.

- No it' s okay, I know why I pain.

She says.

- O, don' t be stupid girl.

I will take you to a doctor a friend of mine.

Take this peel, it will keep you calm.

Vick tells her.

Liza takes the peel.

After a minute se feels dizzy.

They go to building that is out of town in a small road.

They get in.

Mark the doctor of Robert is in the office.

Liza can not realiaze anything.

She is dizzy.

Mark is co operating with vick and punks like him, he earns money from them.

Mark has the envolope that mark has sent to robert is on her office.

Robert had put out of the envolope the peel and the form and kept them to his room as clues in order to put mark in jail.

The envolope has a label on it hat says " unknown resiver ".

Robert resieved the envolope but said the mister morison is dead, so it returned back.

Robert managed to read the form.

He called doctor to examined the peel.

This peel is a medicine that can hypnotize a person and makes him a slave.

Mark hoped that he will take the company of robert.

Mark is entrapped.

She has the advantage of having liza now in front of him.

He could easily make her, her victim.

The two men put liza in the bed.

She is sleeping.

- Well, how can I help?

Mark says and smiles.

- Well I think this girl has a problem.

Vick says.

Mark observes Liza.

- She is pregnant you fool.

He tells him.

- Don' t you think to anything stupid.

Mark tells him.

- I will not help you this time.

I like my freedom.

I am afraid that I will lose it but I intend to delay that.

- What?

Vick says surprised.

- Okay man, you killed me with that.

Vick say.

- Let her for a while here to get some rest.

Mark tells him.

- Okay.

Vick says and goes outside.

Vick calls douglas.

- Man liza is pregnant.

- And what' s the problem?

He replies.

- She has the perfect body and misuraments for our job.

Don' t be emotional kid, you will fail.

Arrange her jobs quickly before her body starts raising.

Don' t be fool.

He says.

- I have already for today.

But I don' t think that she will manage it.

Vick says.

- O come on man, the money is the motivation, tell her about money and she will succeed.

He replies.

- Okay, we will see.

Vick says.

- A don't want this phrase and you know that, boss will be upset, and you know how is the boss.

Douglas says.

- Because I got in the business through you, don' t you think that I cannot do business on my own.

I do all the jobs, unless you want to be alone.

You know that because of the advertisement the girls call me, if you were in this advertisement, you would have done nothing.

Vick says.

- Okay, okay, man, I know that each of us has his role. Never mind, do this that you have to without trace.

  Douglas says.

- Now it' s a deal.

  Vick say.

  Vick gets in the apartment that mark has his office.

  Liza is better.

  Mark has given her a peel so that she could not recognize people.

  Vick takes her and together they go.

  They goes to a hotel near.

  It' noon.

  Vick calls for food, the same time that kevin and allan call for food too.

  Liza should be home at this time.

  Ann calls her.

- Liza hello where have yo been?

- Hello mommy, I am at a job now, can you call me later?

  She says but she looks like drunk.

- Are you fine?

  Ann asks her.

- I could not be more.

  Liza replies.

- Will you come today?

  Alan came today, your father is gone and you are not here, only kevin is here.

- Mom I will be out for a while.

  Kevin says to her mother.

- Ha ha.

  Also kevin will go out.

Liza says and laughs.

- Come home my girl, your dad is missing.

Ann says.

- Was that you wanted mam?

I have heared you several times that you wanted to break up.

Liza says.

- Let me do my life, because when I be sixty years old, like you I will regret for not doing my life.

Liza says.

- I will call you back later.

She continues.

- Okay my girl, buy buy.

Ann replies.

After half an hour Vick and liza start eating.

The time is five o' clock.

- Well your appointment is for ten o' clock.

You have to be ready.

You will be paid very well for that job.

Vick tells liza.

- Okay, but when I will be paid and from whom?

She replies.

- From me as soon as you accomplish the job.

Vick says to her while he eats and smiles.

- You will take some photos and maybe video for a magazine.

Vick tells her.

- Magazine, which magazine?

Liza asks.

- The man that you will see, will notify you.

  Vick says.

- Now you should get some rest and take this peel too.

  It will help you not to have stress.

  You mustn't be nervous at the time of photoshoting.

  Vick says.

- But what about all these peels.

  I think i don' t need them.

  Liza tells him.

- You ought to take them.

  Don' t be stubborn.

  He says and graps her from the hair.

- A, what are you doing.

  Liza shouts.

- A sorry, I would like to get you ready for the role.

  Vick says.

- Which role?

  Liza asks.

- You might participate in a movie.

  This man is a well known producer.

  He says.

- Ooo, I would like to see him.

  Liza says with enthusiasm.

After five hours.

Liza full of lies from vick is going to Planet hotel.

A new five star hotel.

She goes to the room three hundred six.

After one hour she goes.

Douglas who is in the lobby reading a newspaper sees her.

He calls vick.

- Ey, our girl finished the job.

  She is coming to you.

  Vick is outside with the car, he transferred her to the hotel.

- Okay.

  How is she looks?

  Vick ask douglas.

- She looks as if he done for first time.

  We have to train her for the second date.

  We have to do it in the street.

  Douglas says.

- What? Are you crazy?

  She will realize that we take advantage of her.

  Vick says.

- We will do it in a certain district, we will talk to our girls to help her.

  You know what I mean.

  Douglas says.

- Okay see you later, she is coming.

  Vick says.

Liza gets in the vick' s car.

- How was it?

Vick asks.

- I don' t know, it was good, we make a clip photoshooting, but feel a little strange, I feel like I make sex.

She says.

- O you feel that because you liked it a lot, come on lets go to the hotel to tell me more.

Meanwhile.

Robert is calling bob.

- Hello bob.

He says.

- Hello, mister Morison, can you call me in a few minutes, or seconds, it' s okay with me?

He says.

- Okay.

Robert replies.

After a minute Robert calls bob again.

- Hello mister Morison.

I can speak now, there is no problem.

Bob says

- Now you accomplished the assignment I want to tell you something.

Robert says.

- I give you my home that nobody knows that exists.

We don' t need to make the sale with all the papers and stuff, with lawyers and all these, I give to you because I trusted only you.

You have never betrayed me.

If you live inside for some years then you own the house legally according the law.

I give you the home that is among the old bridge and the park in next to the alley, opposite the boulevard.

This that is between the traffic lights and the street lights.

Bob is inside the home at the moment.

He was driving while he received the call from Robert that' s why he got to the home of Robert fast.

- Ooo, sir, it is so kind of you but I don't believe that I worth it.

  I have you as a friend.

  Bob says to him.

- I feel the same with you bob, I 've never had a friend, now that I found it' s late.

  I know that now I cannot be betrayed from a any friend because the years passed for me.

  Robert says.

- Ooo what are you talking about mister Morison?

  Bob asked.

- Go there and ask nothing, continue your life, thank you for your help.

  I want you to know that this home knows the good man and the evil.

  Ha ha.

  It had opened its doors to many people.

Scene

Bob is seating in the big red couch with candles in front of him in the table.

The wooden box with the coins is next to him and he is putting out of it the coins and throwing them inside again.

He is playing with them.

Scene

Meanwhile.

Robert is reading his newspaper.
The column of Gordon.
Max Viewing is in jail.
Jim Cartal, is in jail because had been stilling from a company that he gone after rm.
Mark the doctor as he was calling himself is in jail.
Robert has sent to Mark the police.
They arrested him without a big trial because the clues and the members of jury had agreed that he was to make a crime.

The next morning.
Vick is talking with Douglas.
-   Man that peel that I gave her makes work.

    She wasn' t sure if she made sex or not.

    I have to pay her even though.

    He says.

-   Okay, give her a check, but a check which she can collect after three months.

    Ha ha ha.

    Douglas says.

-   O man you are genius.

    Vick says.

-   Sorry for yesterday man, I talked to you in a bad way, I was a little nervous about liza, I know that she is new for that kind of job.

    Douglas says.

-   Okay man, never mind we know each other since we were kids.

    Tell me about the other thing, the training.

137

Vick tells him.

- Well I have an idea.

  We will take her to a street that we have already spoken to girls that are working there as whores.

  We will tell them not to bother Liza.

  Afterwards we will let her there to think that we will make a clip.

  We will see how many guys will approach her and how she will react.

  Douglas says.

- And if somebody will believe that she works as a whore?

  Vick asks.

- We will be near and we will run to tell him that we are making a film.

  Douglas replies.

- Okay, what about today?

  Vick says.

- No, today, let her go out and give her the check, write five hundred dollars, for after a couple of months.

  Until then we will disappear with all the money she earns.

  Ha ha.

  The producer paid you?

  Douglas says.

- Yes yesterday night after Liza slept I went ant took two thousand.

  Vick says.

Meanwhile

Robert is eating alone.
He has read the weather in his newspaper.
He calls Sean.
Sean is the man who talks too much.
In every situation and job, there is probably one man who like to make comments about others.
This is something that could be good for some reasons.

- Hello Sean, how are you?

  He says.

- Hello mister Morison, I am cleaning the sleeves of the plants.

  Do you want to clean the marbles in the entrance?

  Sean is talking to Robert as if Robert hasn't left.

- No Sean never mind, it will rain in a few minutes.

  He replies.

- How the things are there?

  Robert asks him.

- O sir are you mister Morison? I didn't understand you.

  Kevin told me that he would fix a mop that will help me more with the cleaning mister morison.

  I have been in my village I haven' t seen you since I left.

  He says.

- Don't' call me mister morison, he is dead, I am his brother.

  Robert replies.

- What but when? I am his relative. Who are you?

  Sean says.

- I am his brother.

  Robert says.

- His brother? But nobody knew that he had a brother.

  Sean says.

- Even him didn' t know.

  Robert says.

- It happens for him to learn it by accident, he called me one day to offer me job.

  I was poor and I was sleeping in the parks inside boxes.

  Once I have read that he needed a person for his company.

  As an exterior employee.

I went to his office and he hired me.

Afterwards, from time to time, I saw that we had some common things and habits, for example he disliked gums.

Robert says and has persuaded Sean that Robert is dead.

- You know Robert always had money and always was paying the employees.

Even this month that has a financial problem he found the way to pay them all and as I can know he earned ten thousand dollars more than he expected.

- A okay.

Do you know who took the award of the month?

He had create that in order the employees to have motivation.

Robert says.

- Well, Jenna took it, also she took the price of five hundred award.

Sean says.

- A jenna nice and good girl.

Robert says.

- She was elected in the elections of employees the best employees and they all agreed her to be in charge of building 48.

Sean says.

- A, very nice, this is the most important building. But how they made elections without Robert?

Robert asks.

- Kevin and Robbie decided that.

Sean says.

- Well sean you know all these as you clean and their shoes too, I mean as if you watch them.

Robert says.

- Ha ha, you are right sir.

But what is your name?

Sean says.

- My name is John Morison.

Robert replies.

- What about Liza and Alan?

Robert asks.

- Well Liza is not coming any more.

Alan, I haven't seen him more than you.

The telephone department is not working very well, once I have forgotten my keys inside the company and I was callin half an hour to find someone.

When I eventually found jack, the line was canceled.

I got into company from the rear entrance.

Nobody was there and I saw some plans that they shouldn't be there.

Sean says.

- That' s very bad. There you know is the sector c, there we used to have the plans that were about to be destroyed, but I see that now that robert is dead no one is interested to do that.

Robert says.

- But when he died, does his family know that?

Sean asks.

- He died yesterday.

He was alone in a hotel.

He was left from there so to find a trustful doctor but he couldn't survive.

He died from cancer.

Robert says.

- The half of the drivers had left.

They had complaints from Kevin.

Bad behavior.

- Okay sean thank you for your help.

Robert says.

- I will notify you if I need something else.

Robert says.

- I am sorry for your brother, he was my boss but apart from this he was cousin with my father.

    Sean says.

- I know that Sean, thank you.

    Robert says.

After that call Robert starts thinking.
Robert found that in his lonely he could be happy, he realize that if you know, you can find in a dark room a light, even if it happens to be the screen for the hour in a radio, even if this could be the last thing that he can see when he is about to close his eyes.
The next day.
Robert calls a well known funeral office and arranges the funeral.
- Hello I am brother of Robert Morison, I would like you to arrange his funeral.

    Robert orders the statue of himself in a lying position so to put it into the coffin.

Robert is reading his newspaper, his favorite column.
Carol wife of George wasn't ever found.
- Sean has told everything to everybody.

    He says.

Now all know that Robert is dead. He thinks.
In fact Sean has told all that Robert is alive and the place that he is.
He is enjoying his meal not as it the last one but the first one.
As he thinks that people have to believe.
But Robert had made a mistake.
Sean saw his phone number because Robert called from the hotel
Sean called again in the same number.
The receptionist asks him whom he wanted and...
- E mister Morison please.

    Yes mister Robert Morison.

    The receptionist wasn't notified from Robert and didn't know that he should say that he is dead.

    Robert answers the call.

- Yes it' s me.

    Robert says.

    Sean turns off the phone.

142

\-   The more humen you have in your job the more problems you have.

Sean whispers.

He goes to make plastic surgery.

He has made a plan.

Meanwhile.

Jenna, Robbie and Jack and Kevin and Alan and Ann.

Are in the company.

Kevin has called a detective to tell him what he wants him to do.

After he told him now he waits the detective to call him back.

Kevin told detective that he doesn't have enough money to pay him.

This was a lie, detective had seen the history of Kevin's family and he knows everything about it.

After a few minutes and while detective has thought these the conversation that had with kevin, he calls. Kevin replies. No, but why, but, but let e explain.Detective is not in the line anymore.He refused to search for robert. Kevin says to all Meanwhile Sean before he dows anything goes in theroom that they are all gathered. He gets in. He left a paper sheet in an office. He does it in a very strange way. He doesn' t talk to nobady. He deslikes them all.

Jack sees the little paper. He doesn't know what future will bring for him, but even though he wants to make bad to Robert and now he is pretending that he cares about him.

Meanwhile douglas and vick are preparing the scene for Liza and the job they want to do.

\-   It's a little early for this job. Don't you think?

Vick tells douglas.

\-   We have to be prepared.

Douglas replies.

Both of them are talking to other girls their roles. These girls are models, they think that they are about to make a photo shooting. Vick and Douglas have put barrels with flames on them close to the girls so to show a very dark and adventurous scenery. All the girls wearing a few cloths, very sexy clothes and they have fancy bags. The colors are red, yellow and stars are all over their dresses or shorts they are wearing.

143

Douglas is showing the girls how they must stand. Vick is giving them some last instructions.

- You have to move up to this spot there and come back again here.

He says.

- You have to move and speak very socialy and in a physical way.

Douglas adds.

- Also you have to chew gums.

Vick says.

- Smile to everyone and be friendly enough.

He continues.

Meanwhile liza is calling vick.

- Yes.

He says.

- Well, vick I am afraid to do that. I don't want to stand there. I think something bad will happened to me.

She says.

- O don't be silly, it's your training. You have chosen that. There are no difficulties in that job, you are a woman, it's a piece of cake for a wonderful woman like you. The only thing that you have to do is to stand there and wait so to speak to some people that will approach you. Be prepared for the big life, if you passs this test get ready for the big life, you will know some producers and you may participate in a short movie later.

- Do I have to sleep with them?

- O come on, pretend as they are you boyfriends. Who is going to give you job from these that you used to have as friends, no one. You have the opportunity now. Grap it and don't let the time to pass. You have to be ready at nine o' clock. This street is very crowded but very few approach the girls, only that who are rich. There are all directed, you do not have reason to worry.

- Okay vick, I will come.

- No I will come to pick you up.

Vick switched his cell phone. He breaths out in difficulty.

- I hope she comes.

He says.

- What happened vick?

Douglas tells him.

- Liza told me that she afraid of doing that for tonight. I hope all the thing to go well. You know I have paid the rent for this area and I have to pay the models and the lights and.

- O don't be fool, these models don't need money, they need drugs, we have many to give them.

Douglas says.

- I think she will agree to do it eventually. Have you brought her clothes?

Douglas asks vick.

- Yes.

- You know that you haven't blocked the alley in the corner.

Douglas tells vick.

- Man they asked me three hundred dollars more. I couldn't afford that.

Vick replies.

- Well then we have to keep an eye on that street.

Douglas says.

- Okay. Well we have a lot of free time until the job. Why don't we take advantage of that?

Vick says.

- What do you mean?

Douglas asks him.

- Why don't we taste the models?

Vick says.

- O no man. Wolf has to have his nest clean. If something goes wrong they may go.

Douglas tells him.

- No woman had ever left me man.

Vick says.

145

Vick goes and speaks to the girls while Douglas is going in a shop a few steps far to the spot in order to eat something.

There he finds Angela, a Romanian girl. She has green eyes and big lips red with orange color.

- Hello.

- Hello mister, what could I do for you?

- I would like to have a sandwich please.

- Whit what in it?

- O put everything you want; I only want to see the way that you put.

- O sir, then it's going to be expensive, ha ha.

- As you wish.

  Douglas says.

  Both of them laugh.

  Angela gives the fat sandwich to Douglas.

- Okay thank you.

  He says.

- Here is your receipt.

  Angela tells him.

- Here is your money and my card. What's your name?

  He tells her.

- Angela sir.

  She replies.

- Okay, buy, buy.

  He says.

- Buy buy sir.

  Angela says.

  After Douglas left Angela looked at his card.

  "Manager of artists ".

- Bullshit, he only wants to spend a little nice time.

   She says and throws his card to the garbage.

   Liza is in her bathroom in the hotel. She has filled the bathtub with water.

   She is relaxing in the water and soap.

   She is watching television. She calls Kevin.

- I am naked in the bathtub and I am waiting to have fun with a man.

   She says.

- O you bitch, stop teasing me. Where are you? Don't you wondering about our dad?

   He replies.

- No, I know he is alive and having fun, thing that he had to do many years ago.

   She says.

- I remember the days that the only thing we used to do was to play with te pillows in our room, do you remember?

   She tells him.

- O yeah. Then we got involved with all these business and companies and money.

   He replies.

- Well, I called you because I took a big decision and I don't have any other to talk to.

- O then tell me, we always used to getting on well.

   Kevin tells her.

- I have decided to become a model.

- O that's good I think that was all you wanted in your life.

- Well, yes, but I am anxious about some things, and I am wondering if that was eventually what I wanted.

- What do you mean?

- Well, I will explain you some other time.

- Okay but be careful these jobs are a little wired.

- Okay Kevin buy buy.

   Both of them hung up.

Liza is trying to get up to take her towel, she feels dizzy again.

She falls in the bathtub and hits her head. She stays there unconscious.

The time is passing. Liza starts slipping in the bathtub; the water is near her mouth.

Meanwhile matt is calling Liza. He overtook drugs and he is dying in his apartment.

- Ooh, pick it up.

He says while he is crawling in the floor. Liza cannot hear his cell phone.

After a few minutes the man who is in charge for the room service is knocking the door of Liza's room. Liza doesn't reply. The man is not interested in searching why he doesn't get an answer. He doesn't hear anything from inside. Although he knows that someone is inside because only Vick is outside the room not Liza. He leaves. After a few minutes Vick is getting in the room. While he opens the door he is looking in the next room.

He got there with one of the models that were about to work the evening in the photo shootings.

- Liza, Liza.

Vick says.

- Where the fuck is she?

He continues.

The water in the bathtub had passed her mouth while she is slipping more.

Vick is searching liza all over the room. He eventually goes to the bath. The door is opened. He gets in.

- O damn.

He says.

He pulls her out of the water very carefully. He covers her with a towel.

He doesn't know that she has hit her head. He puts her in the bed.

Liza starts wakening up.

- O my head.

She says.

She pains and she shows that. Vick caresses her in the head.

- What happened?

Vick asks her.

- I slept in the bathroom and hit my head in the edge of the bathtub.

She replies.

- O I see, are you better now?

Vick asks her.

- Yes I am. But I feel a little weak.

She says.

- Yes you have to eat more.

He says to her.

While Vick is helping Liza to get up and get ready he sees some things like woods in her body, like tiny injures.

These signs are signs of hiv, the man that he had slept with in the first date had hiv and now Liza has too. He hadn't used a condom.

Vick doesn't say anything but he knows that signs other girls had died because of hiv and he used to know them until their death.

Meanwhile Christina the model that is in the next room has waken up.

She starts looking for Vick. Vick has given her a peel that made her to lose selfcontrol and also she doesn't know why she is there. She knows that vick brought her but nothing else. Vick had made sex with her.

- Where is he now?

She says.

The room is dark. She turns on a light. She can't find any one.

While Christina is looking for vick, vick has prepared liza for the job.

He is getting her to the point. Vick has left money and a note in the bed of Christina and has written "take the money and go to seatl at my home, I will come tomorrow, there I will make you the queen of models. Yours Vick. "

The time is 20:30. Alan with a friend of him is going to take the car.

- Let's have some fun tonight, I owe that to myself.

Alan says while he gets in the car.

They drive to Las Vegas. There are some events this period of time.

In Vegas there is the photo shooting that Vick and Douglas called that way so to make profit.

The time is 21:20, Douglas is worried. He calls vick.

- Where are you?

- Well liza had an accident and we are on the road now.

- Come quickly because the "one" is coming.

- Who is the one man?

- The clients, man. I call them the one. They feed us.

Both of them hung up.

Liza puts out of her bag a paper sheet and she puts it in her bra without Vick realized her.

Vick and liza go to the meeting point while Christina is reading the note of Vick.

Douglas is looking at them. He approaches vick while vick is parking the car.

- E you know Christina is not here.

- Yes I told her to leave; she wasn't good for that job.

- What are you talking about man? She was black, tall, experienced and pro.

Liza comes and stand next to vick, opposite douglas.

- O come on we have liza now, she is better.

Vick says.

- Liza go and stand next to that girl over there.

Vick tells her.

- O I don't believe you man, you kept the black girl for you.

Douglas says to him.

- O come on man lets'do our job the hour is 22:00.

Vick says.

- Yes okay but before that I want to tell you something.

Douglas says.

- What?

Vick replies.

- Not here come to my van.

Douglas says.

They go toward the van.

Douglas opens the back door.

- From behind ha ha?

Vick says.

Douglsas pulls a military knife from his pocket.

He pushes vick.

- It's better here.

He says.

- This was the last time that you fucked with me.

Douglas says grapes Vick from the mouth and sticks the knife in his back.

Vick is dead.

Douglas covered vick with a rug.

He turns back to the girls.

- Now girls get ready.

He says.

- Action.

He continues.

Meanwhile some cars start to go toward the girls.

The same time Alana and his friend are in a strip show.

Allan is bored.

- O man, all women are same, fake tits, fake eyes, eyelashes and color of hair, let's go, I want ot find a real girl that will give me pleasure.

Alan says.

- Ok man.

His friend replies.

They take the car and they go to an event a few blocks far.

There is a girl that sing.

- Here there are some bitches don't you think?

Friend of alan tells him.

- O no man, here they will meke me tired so to spend a nice time.

He replies.

- A I see, you want something ready.

- Oh yeah now you got it.

They start going to the red light district.

Alan can't drive now, so his friend sits in the drivers seat.

During the route allan is seeing the scenery that vick and Douglas had made.

- O man stop here and turn there. I saw something.

Alan says.

The two men are going to the girls.

- Sslow down a little.

Alan says.

He takes some peels.

Alan has seen the girls and the cars that are near them.

- O man have they changed the red light district here? I wonder.

He says.

He is a little out of control and starts laughing and having a good mood.

The two man approach the girls. They do it through the unblocked alley. Alan rolls down his window and intend to speak to a girl.

Douglas gets up from his chair.

- What is he doing?

He says.

- Ey babe, what can you do to me?

Alan tells to the girl next to Liza.

- Spit you.

She tells him.

Liza wears a fake hair, alan hasn't realized her.

- What?

Alan says in anger.

He pulls a gun through his jacket, he shoots. He was aiming the unknown girl but he killed liza.

The unknown girls had looked the gun and bend a little before Alan shoot.

- O shit man what have you done?

His frined tells him.

- Step on it man let's go.

Alan replies him.

Liza is falling to the ground.

- Oh shit.

Douglas screams. The other girls are leaving screaming.

Alan and his friend are disappearing in the darkness.

After a few minutes police arrived in the point.

Policemen searched the area and found the little paper in Liza's bra that had written "I am pregnant, please save my child".

She has written that as if she knew she would die.

An ambulance has transferred Liza to hospital, the doctors managed to save the baby. The only bad thing was that Liza was pregnant for a little period of time and that she had hiv. The doctors managed to save the baby that wasn't influenced of the disease.

They put the baby to the hospital to help it grow up properly.

After a few meters Alan and his friend had crashed the car. Police bust both of them but friend of Allan was set free. Alan who was the shooter was set to prison time of 2o years. Robert's lawyer said that Alan was drug addicted and didn't want to hurt anybody. The juries decided this penalty for Alan. They also said that a warranty could be given in order Alan gets off the jail.

Ann that was in the trial got crazy, she started to get crazy after he learned about Robert's death but this was the last step of normal life and mind for her. She buried her child and got into a clinic.

Two days has passed, the family of Robert had decided to go to find Robert.

It found where Robert was.

But this is too late.

They found out that Robert lives.

Meanwhile Sean as Robert after the plastic surgery he made enters in the favorite restaurant of Robert Morison.

Robert used to book the table before he gone there. He liked to book the central table next to the aquarium. Sean didn't know that Robert's habit.

Martin is looking at Sean. The plastic surgery has great results but Sean cannot change his voice

- Hello misters Morison how are you?

- Hello, e, e, bring me the most expensive food that you have.

Sean says.

Robert Morison used to eat beefs and the order was already ready because of the many times that Robert has been there.

Martin is a little curious about the behavior of Sean. He calls Alan but his cell phone is switched off. Then he calls Liza, her cell phone is ringing but no one is answering. Her cell phone is covered with sand in the point he was killed.

Afterwards he calls kevin. He answers.

- Hello.

He says.

- Hello Kevin, I am martin from the restaurant. Well, is your dad fine?

He asks him.

- Maybe, he is dead mister martin, haven't you heard that?

Kevin replies.

- But what? What are you talking about?

Martin says.

- Yes, I am going to see it with my eyes.

  Kevin says.

- But your dad is here Kevin, in my restaurant.

  Martin says.

- What? I want to talk to him. Give him to the phone.

  Kevin says.

- Okay, just a moment.

  Mister Morison, mister Morison.

  Martin is calling Sean.

  Sean doesn't realize that because he is not used to his new face yet and to his new role also.

  In the third time that Martin called him Sean gets up.

- What?

  He says to martin.

- E, it's someone on the phone for you.

  Martin says.

  Sean that has fallen in the trap that came up goes to speak to the phone.

- Yes, hello, who is it?

  He says.

- You are Robert Morison?

  Kevin says.

- Well yes I am.

  Sean replies.

- Well you owe me 100.000 dollars sir. i want my money. I have been searching for you many days. Now wait there and I will come.

  Kevin says.

- But, but.

  Sean says.

Sean gives the phone to martin.

- He is not my father. I understood it from the voice.

  Kevin says.

- Well Kevin I was about to tell you that, firstly the different table, afterward the food, then that he didn't know my name and the difference in the voice.

  Martin says.

- Call the police.

  Kevin says.

  Martin and Kevin hung up.

  Sean has left.

- O no.

  Martin says.

He goes to the exit, he looks left and right. He looks cross the road. He sees Sean. He approaches him. Sean realizes that he is followed by martin. Sean goes a little faster. He gets into an alley that is covered with trees.

Martin gets into the alley too. Sean puts out of his jacket a knife and sticks it in the head of martin, between the eyes.

Martin falls dead.

Kevin lied to Sean because he realized that he is a scam. He is traveling to England now to see his dad.

Ann and Alan are with him. Ann have taken peels in order to travel and Alan is for one day free but under police control only to go to see his father.

Meanwhile a man that Robert Morison had fired from his company sees Sean. He thinks that he is Robert Morison. He follows him and when they are in not crowded place the unknown man struggles Sean with a rope.

Later and when the Morison family is back, Kevin learns the truth of Sean.

Meanwhile the funeral of Robert Morison was in the front pages in England.

Robert died from stroke. From that, that he always afraid of, he eat alone and a bone stroked him. He wrote a letter before he died he had it beside him.
He also left his will besides. He left the letter in the table in front of him, after he moved his plate next to him and clean the table while he was sitting there.
He left the will besides the letter. His family got into the room angry, as if it was about to see a robber, not Robert.
The letter said. The life is like you went somewhere on vacations in a hotel.
In your room may all are fine and have calm climate.
In the next room may there is an argument between a couple, in another may
Have sex, you have to face them all as they could happen to your room. I leave my company to Bob, I have sold the house and the yacht.
I have booked the hotel near the house for you to stay as long as you have money until you buy one. Jenna because it wasn't my fault that you father died and because you was a good employee, I give you my company, but to be your own you have firstly to fire jack, he is taking his pension since three years, but I was feeling petty for him, that's why I was having him still in company, he is not feat to your new company, I have written this order in the contract bellow.
And
Robert seems that wanted to write something else but he didn't manage it.
Kevin Morison found another job because he didn't want to work in Robert's company to find money so to pay for Alan to get off the prison.
Ann Morison is in a clinic because she got crazy.
He didn't manage to read in his newspaper the lines above.
Liza Morison is dead.
She used to work as whore for wealthy men. She hasn't realized that she was a whore until her death.
His brother Alan is been interviewed by the police for another crime too, because police men found his block at home.
The same time bob is in the house that Robert told him that he gives to.
He turns the light with one lamp on.
He opens the window.

- Oh what a nice view.

He sais.

- And it's mine and it's free.

He looks a little outside ad he comes back again.

He makes a move but somewhere the floor is rotten, it brakes and bob falls down in the basement.

He is killed.

Now nobody owns this home.

Many people will pass next to it, seeing the open window, they will look at the home. Maybe a robber will be interested to burglar it, many could realize that someone leaves in there, but no one will learn the truth.

maybe in some years someone will find the skeleton of bob.

Meanwhile a little baby is carried by a woman that can not been seen, only her hand can.

This woman is leaving the baby in the steps of an orphanage and is leaving.

The lamp in the home that Bob died, after years of work is burned and switched off.

An evening later someone took the statue of Robert Morison and put it in near the entrance of company.

He has written "even he sleeps he is dangerous".

Many told that he was the creator of the statue many others believed that it was a joke from Robert.

The end.